How to make a fortune with
Options Trading

Samuel Blankson

ISBN: 1-4116-2378-9

Acknowledgement

I give glory to God (for filling my cup to overflowing and guiding me through the valley of the shadow of death), my wonderful wife Uju for making the journey fun and always supporting me, and Chuck Mellon, and Tony Robbins for opening my eyes to the possibilities.

RISK DISCLOSURE STATEMENT

Please read carefully. Futures and Options trading have large potential rewards, but also large potential risk. You must be aware of the risks and be willing to accept them in order to invest in the Futures and Options markets.

DON NOT TRADE WITH MONEY THAT YOU CAN NOT AFFORD TO LOSE.

Contents

Introduction

You may have heard of Options and Futures prior to reading this book but perhaps you have never traded them before. This book shows you how to successfully trade these financial instruments.

The high risk arena that Options belongs has many pitfalls for the beginner, and some seasoned traders have also lost their shirts. So you are wise to be cautious. That's why this book sets out clearly and practically a step by step explanation in layman's terms what Options are how to trade them and how to keep trading them, profitably and safely.

I started trading Options after attending an Anthony Robbins course, "Wealth Mastery" in Frankfurt, Germany. The excellent trainer, Chuck Mellon did his best to impart the required knowledge for trading these financial instruments. I got started immediately and made a small fortune but after the market crash of 2000 I had to re-educate my technique and design better prediction methods and systems that worked in any market.

The years following that have been very exciting and rewarding. In this book I am sharing with you the simple methods I use to create fantastic returns. If you are looking for an Options trading system that works, is simple and gets phenomenal results look no further than this book.

This book is the second of a two part series. Please make sure you read the first book *"How to make a fortune on the Stock Markets"* before continuing with this book.

Chapter 1

- ***Options Contracts***

Options Contracts

If you are like my wife, you like to have the right but not the obligation to buy clothing. Therefore, I find myself being dragged from shop to shop where she will try on clothes, and reserve them behind the counter, so as to be able to return later that day and buy them if she wanted. If after the hours of shopping she has found an alternative to her previously reserved items, she will exercise her right not to buy the reserved items. If she does not find any better replacement, I will find myself being dragged back to the shop where she will exercise her right to buy the reserved clothes. This is a simple analogy of how option trading works.

Investors and speculators buy or sell option contracts that give the buyer the option to buy the underlying equity on, or before an expiry date. Unlike my wife, the option contract buyer has to leave a non-refundable deposit called the premium. The option contract specifies the amount of the agreed underlying equity, the agreed price (also called strike price), and the expiry date of the contract.

There are two types of option contracts, these are the US and European option contracts. The US contract can be exercised (the underlying equity purchased, and the contract closed) anytime before the expiry date, whilst the European contract can only be exercised on the day of the expiry date. (In the US, the expiry date is the third Saturday of the month. As Saturdays are non-market trading days, the expiry date is normally considered the third Friday of the month).

So let us recap:

1. An option is a contract to buy underlying equity.
2. The buyer has the right but not the obligation to exercise (buy) the underlying equity before or on the date of expiry of the contract from the seller.
3. The seller is obliged to sell the underlying equity to the buyer at the agreed price (strike price) before or on the date of expiry (US rules).
4. The price paid for the contract is non-refundable and called the premium.
5. If the option contract is not exercised before or on the date of expiry, the contract expires, and the seller keeps the premium.

There are many expiry dates available per optionable equity contract. Contracts with a long expiry dates are called Long-Term Equity Anticipation Securities (LEAPS). There are many contracts also available for a variety of strike prices per optionable equity. The contract price is calculated by a complex mathematical formula dependent on the time remaining in the contract (due to the expiry date), the strike prices, and their relationship to the current equity price, volatility of the equity price, and the option contract volume.

Thus the further away the strike price is from the actual equity price, the cheaper the contract is. Conversely, the closer the strike price is to the actual price, the more expensive the contract will be. Strike prices can be at any of the following stages:

- Out of the money (furthest away from the actual price, in a direction that is beneficial to the seller).

- Deep in the money (furthest away from the actual price, in a direction that is beneficial to the buyer).
- At the money (at the same price as the actual price).

Types Of Contracts

There are two types of option contracts, as follows:

1.   Call (a long instrument from the buyer's point of view).
2.   Put (a short instrument from the buyer's point of view).

A buyer wanting to benefit from a short trade (where the equity price is falling) would buy a Put contract. The Put option contract increases in price when the underlying equities share price falls.

A buyer wanting to benefit from a long trade (where the equity price is rising) would buy a Call contract. The Call option contract increases in price when the underlying equity share price rises.

As well as a buyer being able to buy Calls and Puts, sellers (also called Contract Writers) can write (sell) Calls and Puts to buyers. The writing of options is more risky than the buying of options, as the former has the writer obliged to sell to the buyer if the buyer exercises their right to buy the underlying security. This will mean the seller would have to first buy the stock at current market prices, and then sell to the buyer at the agreed strike price per the contract. Depending on the agreed strike price, this could be at great loss to the writer.

From the chart in Figure 4-1, you can see the various expectations of the buyers and sellers of option contacts. Let us go through then one by one.

The Call Writer (Call Contract Seller)

The Call writer hopes the underlying equity price stays the same or decreases. He is selling Calls, and Calls buyers want to see the price rise so that the contract value will greatly appreciate. If the underlying equity price stays the same, the buyer will not be able to exercise the option, as they would loose out. As the time to expiry grows shorter, it decreases the price of the contract. If the equity price falls, the Call option will loose value dramatically, thus making it unwise for the buyer to exercise the contract. The seller keeps the premium, and the option contract expires.

If the equity price rises, the exit strategy for the writer is to quickly buy to close the contracts he previously wrote.

The Call Buyer

The Call buyer wants the equity price to rise, increasing the Call option contract price. When that happens, the buyer can do one of two things:

1.   Exercise their Call option contracts.
2.   Sell the now expensive contract on the open market for profit.

If the equity price falls, the exit strategy for the buyer is to sell to close their contracts.

The Put Writer (Put Contract Seller)

The Put writer wants the underlying equity price to stay the same or rise. This is because he/she is writing Puts. The buyer of the Put wants to see the price fall so that the contract value will greatly appreciate. If the underlying equity price stays the same, the buyer will not be able to exercise the option, as he would loose out. As the time to expiry grows shorter, it decreases the price of the contract. If the equity price rises, the Put option will loose value dramatically, thus making it unwise for the buyer to exercise the option. The writer keeps the premium, and the option contract expires.
If the equity price falls, the exit strategy for the writer is to quickly buy to close the contracts that they previously wrote.

The Put Buyer

The Put buyer wants the equity price to fall, therefore increasing the price of their Put option contract. When that happens, the buyer can do one of two things:

1.   Exercise their Put option contracts.
2.   Sell the now expensive contract on the open market for profit.

If the equity price rises, the exit strategy for the buyer is to sell to close their contracts.

Note that selling executed by a buyer is not the same as the writing carried out by a seller. The former passes the responsibility of ownership for a contract to another buyer, whilst the latter creates a contract.

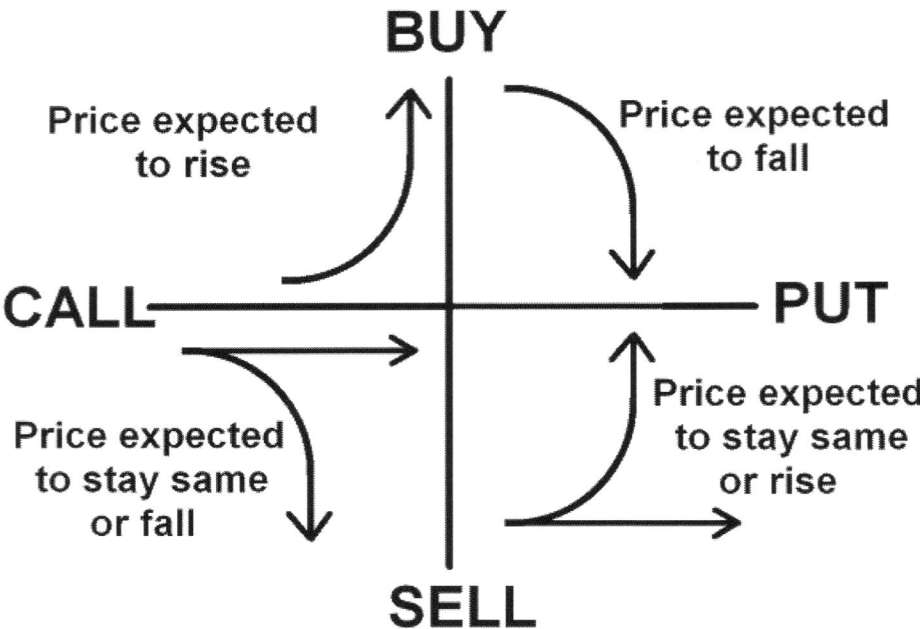

Figure 4-1: Option contract expectation chart

There are many ways to play options. We will not cover all of them in this volume, as they are not all appropriate or simple enough for the beginner. For those of you interested in delving deeper, you can investigate further at the Optionetics site *http://www.optionetics .com/education/trading.asp*.

Nudity In Options Writing

When you write options against equity that you do not own, you are said to be going naked. Doing this exposes you to potential losses that could exceed your momentum investment allocation. Due to the increased risk of writing naked options, I strongly advice you do not write naked Calls or naked Puts.

To explain this further, let us say that you wrote 10 Call contracts for October $5 on TFF (stock symbol for an imaginary company called Total Financial Freedom Corporation). When you wrote the contracts, TFF's equity price was $7. Now leading up to the October expiry date, the stock has risen in price to $60 in the 6 months. You are exercised.

That means you have to go buy 10 multiplied by the number of shares per contract (normally 100), multiplied by the option price $60, less commission charges (which for this simple example we will assume is $20).

$$(10 \times 100 \times \$60) - \$20 = \$59,980$$

You would then sell these stocks, as you are obliged, to the buyer for the agreed $5 as per the contract strike price. This would be 10 multiplied by the number of shares per contract (normally 100), multiplied by the option price $5, less commission charges (which for this simple example we will assume is $20).

$$(10 \times 100 \times \$5) - \$20 = \$4,980$$

This will leave you out of pocket by $54,960. Do you see why I am advising you as a beginner, NOT to go naked?

Sellers of contracts only get the premium. On the other hand, buyers of options get more when it works out, but only loose their premium when it does not work out. Because of this, I will only advise, and cover buying options and selling Covered Calls in this book. See *www.investopedia.com* or *www.Optionetics.com* websites for further information on writing options if you are still interested.

Let us now look at how to make some serious money with a small amount through buying options contracts.

First things first, asset allocation (see Appendix 3 for more information). Make sure you are not exceeding your allocation for momentum investments. Divide your momentum allocation into three equal amounts, and assign one third towards options trading. Remember that your momentum allocation should never exceed 20%, no matter how rich you are. Only use 5% to 10% of your total investment funds.

Just to correct any false over optimistic thoughts you have about options trading, imagine you have lost all your option-trading investments. How would you feel? Go back and look at the percentage you allocated to momentum, are you prepared to loose this amount? If you could not do without it, then reduce the amount you are allocating to momentum investments.

Chapter 2

- **Covered Calls**

Covered Calls

When you own the underlying equity, you can write Call contracts against that equity. This is called Writing a Covered Call. Your risk with a Covered Call is limited to your own equity. This strategy is great if you want to extend gains on your equity. Let us look at this strategy in detail.

Covered Call Technique

The best way to use Covered Calls is as a hedge against falling stock prices. You can use the following techniques (covered in detail in *How to make a fortune on The Stock Markets*), if you buy a stock and you want to stay in it for the long term, but also want protection against the corrections that naturally will occur. These techniques are to use Fibonacci, Elliot Wave analysis and Candlestick signalling, to write Covered Calls during an Elliot Wave correction (Elliot Wave 5 to Elliot Wave C). You will know when you have reached Elliot Wave C, because you can calculate it with the Fibonacci 61.8% line equation.

High – ((High – Low) x 0.618) = Upward trending Fibonacci 61.8% line

Low – ((High – Low) x 0.618) = Downward trending Fibonacci 61.8% line

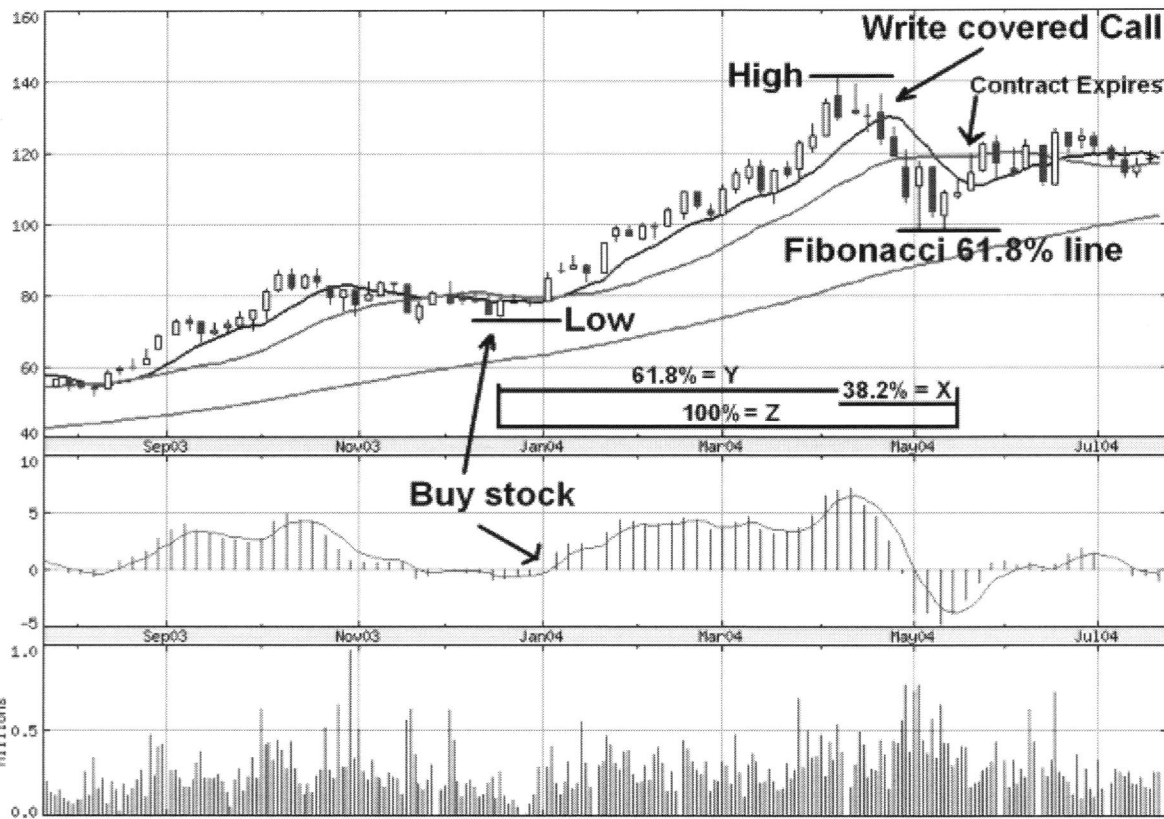

Figure 4-2: Trading Covered Calls with Elliot Wave and Fibonacci

You can use the Upward Trending Criteria to select stocks to trade this technique. As you can see from the chart in Figure 4-2, you buy the stock when the 20 and 50-day Moving Average (MA) diverge from each other. The 20-day MA should be above the 50-day MA. When you see three black candlesticks following each other, write a Covered Call for the equity. Calculate where the Fibonacci 61.8% line will occur.

To calculate the correct expiry date, measure the advancing section of the chart (from Elliot Wave C to Elliot Wave 5). Once you have this length, you can calculate the length of the correction by the following equation:

If X = correction phase length
and
Y = advancing phase length

Total cycle length = Z = X + Y

Z = Y / 0.618
X = Y / 0.618 - Y

Similarly, if you only knew the corrective phase length (X), and wanted to calculate the equation for Y (the advancing phase length), it would be:

$$Y = X / 0.382 - X$$

This is important for determining the length of time over which to write the Covered Call. Be warned that its effectiveness decreases exponentially with decreasing volume and decreasing market cap. Therefore, you will find it most accurate when used with the indexes, big volume stock, and large cap stock.

Further Profits With The Covered Call Technique

You can lock in more profits by buying a Call at Elliot Wave C, and selling to close the Call option at Elliot Wave 5, before you write the Covered Call. This way, you are making a large gain on your Call option, and a respectable gain on your equity price appreciation. When the stock reverses for the correction, you will be able to hedge the equity price losses with the Covered Call gains.

As you work with a group of stocks and indexes (QQQQ, DIA, SPY), you will develop a feel for their patterns, and the best expiry date lengths to apply. For large caps and indexes, this is roughly two to four months. You can also apply this technique with stocks from the following screeners:

- The Good Man (aka The Upward Trended)[1]

---

[1] The Good Man (aka The Upward Trended), represents upward trended stock, and is explained in detail in *The Practical Guide to Total Financial Freedom: Volume 3.*

Field Name	Operator	Value
% Price Change YTD	>=	20
Next Yr Growth Rate	>=	25
Rev Growth YTD vs YTD	>=	20
Net Profit Margin	>=	10
Return on Equity	>=	15
12-Month Relative Stren...	>=	80
P/E Ratio: Current	>=	2

Figure 4-3: Criteria for Upward Trending Stocks

Use *http://moneycentral.msn.com/investor/finder/customstocks.asp* to access the screener. Key in the details in Figure 4-3 and click Run Search.

- The Flyer (aka The High Volume Lift)[2]

Field Name	Operator	Value
Last Volume	>=	5*Avg. Daily Vol. Last 2 Weeks
Last Price	>=	10
Market Capitalization	>=	1,000,000,000
Last Volume	>=	1,000,000

Figure 4-4: Criteria for The flyer based on dramatic volume increase

---

[2] The Flyer (aka The High Volume Lift), represents a stock price move from the Elliot Wave 4 to 5 position, or a single day price surge, and is explained in detail in *The Practical Guide to Total Financial Freedom: Volume 2.*

Field Name	Operator	Value
Previous Day's Closing Price	>=	52-Week High
3-Month Relative Strength	>=	60
Avg. Daily Vol. Last Year	>=	10,000
Previous Day's Closing Price	>=	10

Figure 4-5: Criteria for The flyer based on 52-week high

Use *http://moneycentral.msn.com/investor/finder/customstocks.asp* to access the screener. Key in the details in Figure 4-4 and Figure 4-5 then click Run Search.

- The Marketers (aka The Indexes)[3]

These are mainly QQQQ (NASDAQ), SPY (S & P), and DIA (Dow Jones Industrial Average).

Exit Strategy For Covered Call Technique

From time to time, you may miscalculate the Elliot Wave cycle. When this happens, you could be surprised with a sudden unexpected drop in price. Apply the exit strategy if the stock drops over 10% in price in a single day, or goes through three consecutive days of black candlesticks (three days in a row where the stock closed lower than the open price). If you need to exit out of the Covered Call because the price is reversing unexpectedly, you still need to Buy to Close the Covered Call contracts. You may make a loss, but not as much as if you stayed in and were exercised.

You will need to set up alerts to monitor the stock. Set the alerts to email or page you if the price changes by 5% in a day.

DO NOT USE STOP ORDERS FOR OPTIONS TRADING. The market makers love these orders, as they can make extra profits by executing your order at a convenient price for them, and an inconvenient one for you. The reason you do not even want to use stop limit orders, is that often the market makers can move the option prices to their advantage, mopping up orders that are near the market price in the name of volatile price movement. The options market is also very volatile and there are regular price spikes. Do not get caught out by one of these.

I once placed a limit order to buy an option contract for half the market price. Checking on it a couple of hours later, I saw that it had been filled. I immediately sold it and made 100% profit. I hoped the Call writer learned the important lesson never to use market

---

[3] The Marketers (aka The Indexes), represent indexes, funds and ETFs, and are *explained in detail in of* The Practical Guide to Total Financial Freedom: Volume 2.

or stop market orders when trading options. Do not let this happen to you. Only use limit orders with options.

Chapter 3

- ***Techniques For Buying Options Profitably***

Techniques For Buying Options Profitably

I like simplicity in my investing techniques. I find that the simple techniques are the best, so here I have four simple techniques for buying options safely and profitably. You will need an account with a reputable broker. See Appendix 1 for a list of online brokers.

Take your time and learn your broker's online trading platform first, before placing any live option trades. Wire or transfer funds (a third of your momentum allocation) into your account, whilst rereading all supporting material on your account limits and rules, so that you understand the risk implications of trading options. Once you have familiarised yourself with the brokers systems, you are ready to place your first trade.

When selecting what strike price to buy, always select two strike prices away, unless the equity price is less than $12.50. This will get you a better balance of price to performance. With Calls, this will be the next strike price up, and with Puts, this will be the next strike price down, see
Figure 4-10.

The Elliot Wave Climb Technique

In this technique, you buy a Call at Elliot Wave analysis point C (Elliot Wave C) and sell at Elliot Wave 1, wait for Elliot Wave 2 to buy a Call, and Sell to Close at Elliot Wave 3. Again, you wait until Elliot Wave 4, then buy a Call, and Sell to Close at Elliot Wave 5. Finally, you buy a Put at Elliot Wave 5. Using Fibonacci, calculate the 38.2% line, 61.8% line, and the correction phase length. Place a limit order to sell to close your Put at the Fibonacci 38.2% line. Wait until Elliot Wave B, then buy another Put option, this time wait until the equity hits the Fibonacci 61.8% line, then Sell to Close the Put option.

Use *http://moneycentral.msn.com/investor/finder/customstocks.asp* to access the screener. Key in the details in Figure 4-6 then click Run Search.

Field Name	Operator	Value
Previous Day's Closing Price	>=	0.7*52-Week High
3-Month Relative Strength	>=	95
Avg. Daily Vol. Last Year	>=	1,000,000
Previous Day's Closing Price	<=	52-Week High
Previous Day's Closing Price	>=	20

Figure 4-6: Criteria for Upward trending personalities

Field Name	Operator	Value
% Price Change YTD	>=	20
Next Yr Growth Rate	>=	25
Rev Growth YTD vs YTD	>=	20
Net Profit Margin	>=	10
Return on Equity	>=	15
12-Month Relative Strength	>=	80
P/E Ratio: Current	>=	2

Figure 4-7: Criteria for Upward Trending Stocks

Use *http://moneycentral.msn.com/investor/finder/customstocks.asp* to access the screener. Key in the details in Figure 4-7 and click Run Search.

Field Name	Operator	Value
Last Volume	>=	5*Avg. Daily Vol. Last 2 Weeks
Last Price	>=	10
Market Capitalization	>=	1,000,000,000
Last Volume	>=	1,000,000

Figure 4-8: Criteria for The flyer based on dramatic volume increase

Field Name	Operator	Value
Previous Day's Closing Price	>=	52-Week High
3-Month Relative Strength	>=	60
Avg. Daily Vol. Last Year	>=	10,000
Previous Day's Closing Price	>=	10

Figure 4-9: Criteria for The flyer based on 52-week high

Use *http://moneycentral.msn.com/investor/finder/customstocks.asp* to access the screener. Key in the details in Figure 4-8 and Figure 4-9 then click Run Search.

You can use this technique for years on the same small group of stocks. The benefit of doing this is that you will get to know the stock personality intimately, therefore making it easier to predict Elliot Wave movements and Fibonacci lines.

Remember to keep an eye on the long term Elliot Wave movement as a reversal in the macro range will cause all the micro Elliot Wave cycles to reverse. Always look at the largest range charts first to determine the macro cycle, then work your way in towards a year, or six-month chart.

Always buy two strike prices from the actual equity price at time of buying the options. See
Figure 4-10, for an example of how the price varies greatly from the current equity price. In Figure 4-10, the areas of dark shading are contracts deep in the money.

Calls							Strike Price	Puts						
Symbol	Last	Change	Bid	Ask	Volume	Open-Int		Symbol	Last	Change	Bid	Ask	Volume	Open-Int
UDBHD.X	8.30	▼0.20	7.40	7.80	10	44	20.00	UDBTD.X	0.25	▲0.05	0.05	0.25	32	267
UDBHX.X	6.50	0.00	5.10	5.60	0	13	22.50	UDBTX.X	0.45	▲0.10	0.25	0.50	103	635
UDBHE.X	3.60	▼0.60	3.30	3.60	62	336	25.00	UDBTE.X	0.90	▲0.30	0.80	1.05	465	879
UDBHY.X	2.05	▼0.65	2.00	2.00	298	881	27.50	UDBTY.X	1.85	▲0.50	1.85	2.05	443	216
UDBHF.X	0.95	▼0.40	0.85	1.05	961	2,044	30.00	UDBTF.X	3.40	▲0.55	3.30	3.60	22	99
UDBHZ.X	0.40	▼0.10	0.30	0.55	82	460	32.50	UDBTZ.X	4.80	▲0.20	5.20	5.60	50	8
UDBHG.X	0.35	▲0.05	0.05	0.30	10	106	35.00	UDBTG.X	0.00	0.00	7.50	7.90	0	0
UDBHU.X	0.25	▲0.05	N/A	0.25	20	1	37.50	UDBTU.X	0.00	0.00	9.90	10.30	0	0
UDBHH.X	0.15	0.00	N/A	0.25	0	25	40.00	UDBTH.X	12.70	▲1.10	12.20	13.00	15	0

Options Expiring Fri, Aug 20, 2004

Figure 4-10: Option price variance around equity price ($26.50)

Alternatives To The Elliot Wave Climb Technique

It is not always easy to spot Elliot Wave 1 through Elliot Wave 5. Elliot Wave C and Elliot Wave 5 are easy to spot because they precede major price reversals. The other waves in between however, can be blurred. Because of this, many of you might wish to buy a LEAP or a longer expiry dated Call option, and stay in it from Elliot Wave 1 until Elliot Wave 5. Then buy a Put contract, calculate the Fibonacci 61.8% line, and set a limit order to Sell to Close the Put option at the Fibonacci 61.8% line. This is much simpler.

Fibonacci Bounce

Because you can calculate Elliot Wave A and Elliot Wave C accurately, you can use a Put to benefit from them. Remember Elliot Wave 5 is over as soon as you see three black candlesticks in three consecutive days. Once you see this you know it is safe to buy a Put, because the stock is heading for Elliot Wave A, which will end at the Fibonacci 38.2% line (0.381966011250105, precisely). Once this price has been reached, sell to close your Put option, and wait for Elliot Wave C where you can sell to close the Put option.

Avoid buying a call to benefit from the rise to Elliot Wave B from Elliot Wave A, as this is often very short lived and difficult to time. When the stock is in an upwardly trending pattern, Elliot Wave A to Elliot Wave B often occurs the same day.

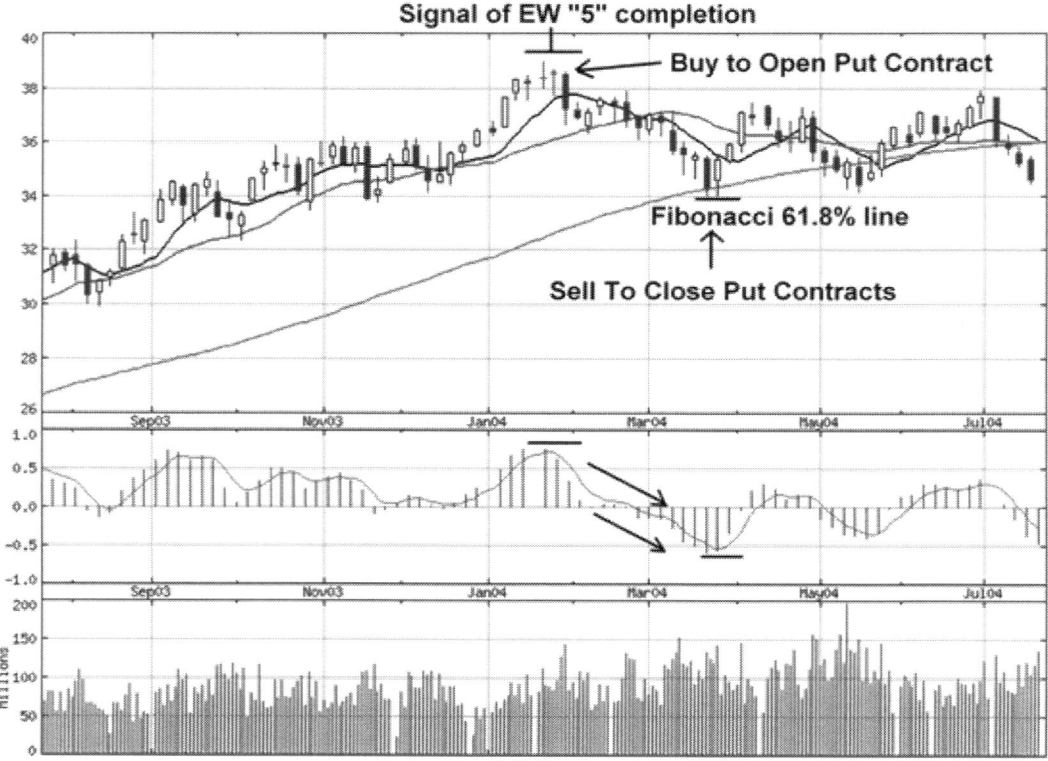

Figure 4-11: Trading Puts with Fibonacci 61.8% line

Figure 4-11 shows you how to identify the end of an Elliot Wave advancement (Elliot Wave 5). You will see that for four days in a row, there are black candlesticks, which signal Elliot Wave 5 completion. You can buy the Put after this signal. Note that Elliot Wave A was barely one day long. This would have been very difficult to profit from. This trade would have earned you 10.5% if you sold short, but with options, you would have earned over 100%. The ratio of option price growth in relation to equity price movement is 10:1 if the strike price was out of the money by one or two strike prices. This is a rough figure; often it is more, and at other times, it is less. Volume and time to contract expiry play a huge part in this price.

Puts, Puts And More Puts

You can use the principles discussed previously to trade downwardly trending stocks. For downwardly trending stock, you need to return to the Bad Man screeners which is covered in detail in *How to make a fortune on the Stock Markets* and briefly reiterated in Appendix 2. Let us recap.

Stepping Put Technique

You can find stocks like these by going to Moneycentral, and keying in the following criteria into the deluxe stock screener at, *http://moneycentral.msn.com/investor/finder /customstocks.asp.* Key in the details in Figure 4-12, Figure 4-13, and Figure 4-14, then click Run Search.

Field Name	Operator	Value
% Price Change YTD	<=	20
Next Yr Growth Rate	<=	20
Rev Growth YTD vs YTD	<=	20
Net Profit Margin	<=	20
Return on Equity	<=	20
12-Month Relative Stren...	<=	20
ROI: 5-Year Avg.	<=	20
Avg. Daily Vol. Last Year	>=	1,000,000

Figure 4-12: Criteria for Downward Trending Stocks

Field Name	Operator	Value
% Price Change YTD	<=	20
Next Yr Growth Rate	<=	20
Rev Growth YTD vs YTD	<=	15
Net Profit Margin	<=	20
Return on Equity	<=	20
12-Month Relative Stren...	<=	20
ROI: 5-Year Avg.	<=	20
Avg. Daily Vol. Last Year	>=	100,000
50-Day Moving Average	<=	200-Day Moving Average
% Price Change YTD	<=	-30

Figure 4-13: Criteria for 200-day MA breakers

Field Name	Operator	Value
% Price Change YTD	Display Only	
Avg. Daily Vol. Last Year	>=	1,000,000
Previous Day's Closing Price	>=	0.2*200-Day Moving Average
Previous Day's Closing Price	<=	0.7*200-Day Moving Average
Last Price	>=	10
% Price Change Today	<=	-1

Figure 4-14: Criteria for 200-day MA deep divers

The criteria in Figure 4-12, Figure 4-13, and Figure 4-14 will help you harvest a list of downward trending stocks. These share prices are falling rapidly. Let us look at one of them in detail.

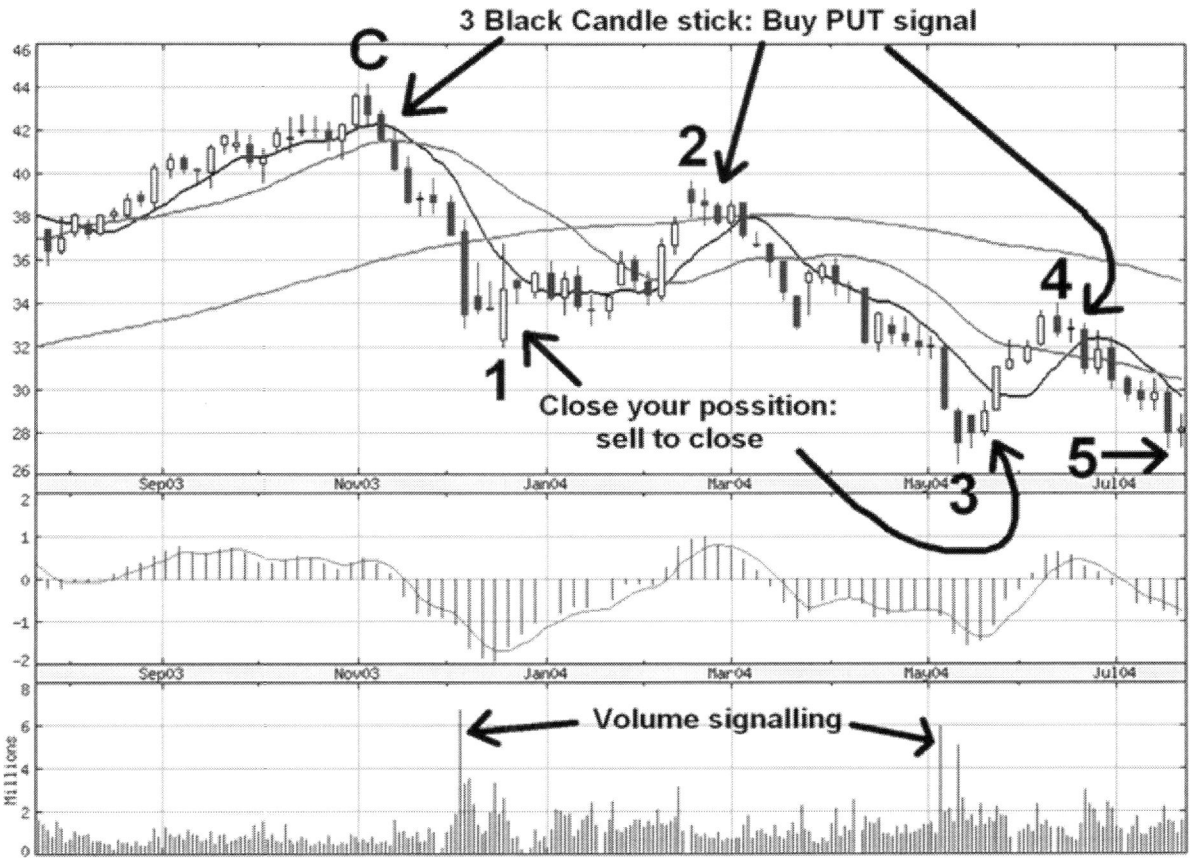

Figure 4-15: Trading Put options using Elliot Wave and Candlestick signalling

You can see in Figure 4-15 that the appearance of three black candlesticks was used to signal buying the Puts. I then sell them when I have made 100% profit, or as soon as two white candlesticks appear, or the distribution between days with white candlesticks and days with black candlesticks become 50-50. What do I mean? Well note that from Elliot Wave C to Elliot Wave 1, there are hardly any white candlesticks. After Elliot Wave 1, white and black candlesticks appear interchangeably. That is what I mean. When every other candlestick is a different colour, it is time to sell to close the Put positions.

I also use volume signalling to warn me about upcoming major price reversals. Note that preceding every major price reversal, that a week or two prior to it, there was a volume spike. When you see a volume spike, prepare to sell at the next advantageous price within the next five trading days.

Using this technique, you should be able to double your money every two to four months. Remember that as long as you bought your option at one or two strike prices away, every 10% fall in the equity price, will see your Put option doubling in its price.

Using Fibonacci For Puts

You can use upward trending stock to trade Puts if they have reached their Elliot Wave 5 point. In Figure 4-16, you see the three-candlestick signal. Also, note that the price has dropped below the previous low to the Fibonacci 38.2% line. From Elliot Wave analysis, you know that this is Elliot Wave A, so it must rise again to Elliot Wave B. The price at Elliot Wave B is the price you are going to pay for your Put. Once you buy your Put, wait until the price approaches the Fibonacci 61.8% line before Selling to Close the Put option.

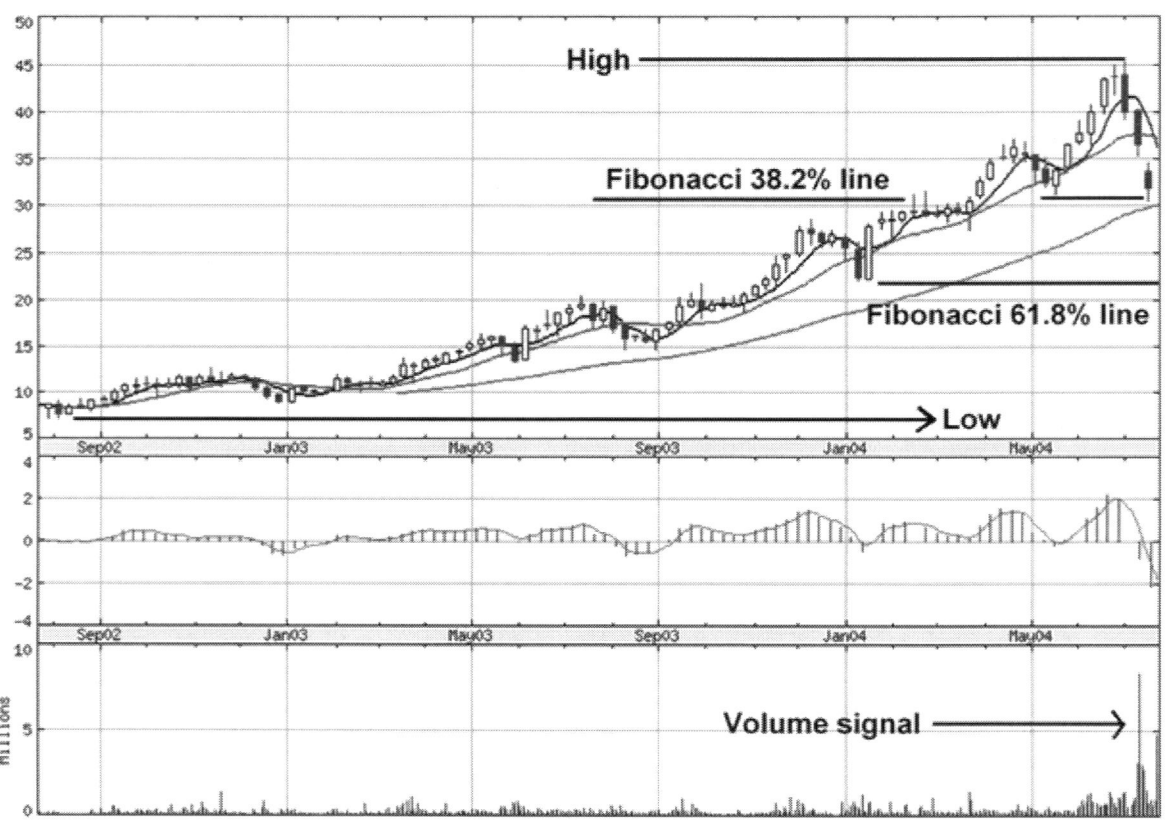

Figure 4-16: Trading price corrections with Fibonacci

Field Name	Operator	Value
Today's Low Price	<=	0.9*Previous Day's Closing Price
Last Price	>=	20
Market Capitalization	>=	50,000,000
Last Volume	>=	1,000,000

Figure 4-17: Criteria for selecting single day price downward spikes

Use *http://moneycentral.msn.com/investor/finder/customstocks.asp* to access the screener. Key in the details in Figure 4-17, then click Run Search.

Your exit strategy is to Sell to Close the Put position if you misjudged the trade and start loosing money. This technique can only fail if you calculated the Fibonacci lines incorrectly, stayed in the option after Elliot Wave C had been reached in the equity price, or you did not use the three black candlestick signalling.

There is a lot more you can learn about options trading. We have only covered the essential information required for making four digit percentage returns annually from options trading.

This section of the book concentrated on getting you to know the essential money making information. Further useful information for a beginner and educational options links are listed below, for you to complete your education. The more general information on opening accounts, funding your account and such, can also be obtained from the following links.

- *http://www.optionetics.com*
- *http://biz.yahoo.com/opt*
- *http://www.ino.com/*
- *http://www.schaeffersresearch.com/*
- *http://www.amex.com/*
- *http://www.888options.com/learning/getting_started.jsp*
- *http://www.optionsxpress.com/*
- *http://www.investopedia.com/*
- *http://www.tradingacademy.com/optionstrading.shtm*

Conclusion

Options trading can be volatile and risky if you do not know what you are doing or if you are not following a proven entry and exit strategy along with a good asset allocation plan (see Appendix 3 for more information). This book teaches you how to build on your knowledge from the first book, *How to make a fortune on the Stock Markets*. By mastering profitable stock trading from *How to make a fortune on the Stock Markets*, you can progress to use this book to trade optionable stocks. You will now know how to buy Calls and Puts and use Covered Calls, to maximise your returns. You will also know how to use Fibonacci lines, Elliot Wave theory, MACD as well as moving averages to accurately predict stock movement so as to correctly predict sentry and exit points in your options trades. The system and techniques discussed in this book are so simple that anyone can use them to successfully trade options and make double and triple figure annual returns.

It is my wish that you apply asset allocation (see Appendix 3 for more information) to your investment funds and use 5% to 10% of this fund to invest in stock options using the strategies covered in this book. If you follow the advise and techniques highlighted in this book you too will see great yields from your options portfolio.

RISK DISCLOSURE STATEMENT

Please read carefully. Futures and options trading have large potential rewards, but also large potential risk. You must be aware of the risks and be willing to accept them in order to invest in the futures and options markets. **DO NOT TRADE WITH MONEY THAT YOU CANNOT AFFORD TO LOSE.**

-

Appendices

Appendix 1

Online Broker List

- **A.B. Watley** – *www.abwatley.com.* Offers NASDAQ II real-time quotes and trades, from $10.
- *Accutrade – www.accutrade.com.* $30 per trade up to 1000 shares. Online trading requires free proprietary software. Also offers mutual funds and options trading. Margin rate is 1-2% above the brokerage call rate. $5000 minimum account balance. One notable feature is the ability to place trades at a future time when specific conditions are met. Compatible with Sharp's Zaurus PDA.
- **AFTrader** – *www.aftrader.com.* $9.95 per trade, wireless trading at no extra charge, free news alerts, free premium research, no fee IRAs, and free unlimited real-time quotes.
- **American Express Brokerage** – *http://br1.americanexpress.com/amex/ bu/fd/cda/ main/0,1484,L-2,00.asp.* $14.95 per trade for up to 3000 shares. Also offers mutual funds trading. No minimum account balance. News, quotes, alerts, company research, S&P MarketScope, and Comtex are included.
- **Ameritrade** – *http://www.ameritrade.com.* $8 per market orders, $13 per limit orders. Also options, mutual funds, and bonds.
- **Amerivest** – *http://www.amerivestinc.com*
- **Atlantic Financial** - *http://www.atlanticfinancial.com*
- **Bidwell & Co.** – *http://www.bidwell.com/.* Starting at $12 per trade.
- **Boom** – *http://www.boom.com.* Hong Kong.
- **Brown & Co**. – *http://www.brownco.com.* Cheapest. $5 per trade for market orders, $10 per trade for limit orders. 100 real time quotes per trade. They only want investors with five years of experience.
- **Brunswick Direct** – *http://www.brunswickdirect.com.* Focused solely on 22 emerging markets.
- **Burch & Company** – *http://www.thetradersclub.com.* Fees from $9.95 to $14.95.
- **Bush Burns** – *http://www.bushburns.com.* $25 per trade.
- **Charles Schwab** – *http://www.schwab.com.* Allows you to buy and sell stocks, mutual funds, options, and treasuries. $30 trades up to 1000 shares, or 3 cents a share for more than 1000 shares. They also offer 50 real-time quotes per trade, plus research from Credit Suisse First Boston, Hambrecht, and Quist for $30 per month. $5000 minimum account balance.
- **Citibank** – http://www.citibank.com. Online banking and trading.
- **CompuTEL** – *http://www.computel.com.* $9 per trade for market orders for 1000 to 5000 shares, one cent per share additional over 5000 shares. $19 per trade for limit orders. Also options. 100 free real time quotes per day. No-fee IRAs. $5000 minimum opening balance.

- **Credit Suisse First Boston Australia Equities Private Limited** – *http://www. csfbaep.com.au.* Australia.
- **CyberCorp** – *http://www.cybercorp.com/default.asp.* Online broker that caters to active traders. Subsidiary of Schwab.
- **Datek** – *http://www.datek.com.* $10 per NASDAQ and NYSE trades. Unlimited real time quotes. 1-minute order execution or it is free. In addition, you can set price limits for your stocks and they will email you when the conditions are met. $2000 minimum account balance.
- **Delta Equity Services** – *http://www.deltaequity.com.* $35 plus half a percent of the total amount.
- **D.F. Mainland Group** – *http://www.dfmainland.co.nz.* New Zealand.
- **Discover Brokerage Direct** – *http://www.discoverbrokerage.com.* $15 per trade. Also offers mutual funds, options, and bond trading (including treasuries). Fee-based package adds research from Morgan Stanley, news, real time quotes, and portfolio management. Margin rate is 0.75 to 2.5% above the brokerage call rate. $2000 minimum account balance.
- **CSFB Direct** – *http://www.csfbdirect.com.* $20 per trade for up to 1000 shares. Also options, bonds and mutual funds. No minimum account balance. Excellent information package including S&P MarketScope, Zacks analyst recommendations, 100 real time stock and option quotes per trade, Reuters market news, and Lipper mutual fund researChâteau. Also, research from Donaldson Lufkin Jenrette. Integration with pagers and handhelds.
- **Dreyfus** – *http://www.edreyfus.com.* $15 per trade (first three trades are free). Best rate on options: $1.75 per contract with a $15 minimum. Real-time quotes when ordering. Margin rate is 0.5 to 1% above the brokerage call rate. $1000 minimum account balance, $2000 for margin accounts.
- **EquityStation.com** – *http://www.equitystation.com.* Caters to active investors. $19.95 market orders for 1-99 trades a month, $16.95 per trade for 100-299 trades a month, and $14.95 per trade for 300+ trades a month (price change is retroactive).
- **EmpireNow.com** – *http://www.lowfees.com.* $7 for market orders, $12 for limit orders. Market orders of 1000+ shares of stocks above $5 per share are commission-free. Also options, bonds and mutual funds. No minimum balance.
- **E*TRADE** – *http://www.etrade.com.* $15 per trade for up to 5000 shares on market orders of listed stocks, $20 for unlisted stocks and limit orders up to 5000 shares. Includes portfolio tracking system (with alerts), current market data, candlestick charts, and other technical analysis tools. Real-time quotes $30 per month. Also offers options and bonds. $5 to talk to a live broker. Margin rate: 1.75-2.25% over brokerage call rate. $1000 minimum account balance, $2000 for margin accounts. The site also includes a trading demo so you can see how everything works. Some access to IPOs at the offering price.

- **Fidelity** – *http://personal.fidelity.com/trade/index.html*. $29 per trade for up to 1000 shares. Unlimited real time quotes. Investment research from Salomon Smith Barney, plus access to IPOs.
- **Fifth Third Bank** – *http://www.53.com*
- **TheFinancialCafe.com** – *http://www.financialcafe.com*. Free market order electronic trades, $4.95 limit order electronic trades, online banking, mortgage, and insurance.
- **First Discount Brokerage** – *http://www.1db.com*. Offers full service, discount, and online brokerages services.
- **Firstrade** – *http://www.firstrade.com*. $10 per order, $5 per NASDAQ order over 1000 shares.
- **FreeTrade.com** – *http://www.freetrade.com*. Free equity trades, $5 stop and limit orders.
- **FREETRADEZ** – *http://www.freetradez.com*. Online broker offering 100% commission free trades (ad-based revenue).
- **Freedom Investments** – *http://www.freedominvestments.com*. $15 per trade.
- **Freeman Welwood** – ***http://www.freemanwelwood.com***. $15 per trade for market orders, $20 per trade for limit orders up to 2000 shares. Above 2000 shares are one cent per share.
- **GE Financial Brokerage** – *http://www.gefn.com/gebrokerage/index .html*
- **Global Access** – *http://www.globefin.net*. NASDAQ Level II trading as low as $9.95 for unlimited shares.
- **Harris InvestorLine** – *http://www.harrisinvestorline.com*. $13 per trade for market orders, $18 per trade for limit orders.
- **Hoyou Barnes NetInvestor** – *http://www.netinvestor.com*. Commissions are $19 + $0.01 per share. In addition, mutual funds, bonds, options, and CDs. Portfolio tracking, news, and researChâteau $5000 minimum account balance.
- **Interactive Broker** – *http://www.interactivebrokers.com*
- **INTLTRADER.com** – *http://www.intltrader.com*. Trades in foreign and domestic securities.
- **Investex Securities Group** – *http://www.investexpress.com*. $15 per trade for most trades. Also mutual funds, options, and bonds. No minimum account balance.
- **InvestIN** – *http://www.investin.com*. $10 per trade. Free real-time quotes.
- **InvestorLine** – *http://www.investorline.com*. $25 per trade for market orders. From the Bank of Montreal. Also mutual funds.
- **InvesTrade** – *http://www.investrade.com*. $8 per trade for stocks. Automated touch-tone phone trading at the same price. An options trade is charged at $1.75 per contract, $15 minimum.
- **Jack White & Co** – *http://www.jackwhiteco.com*. Commissions start at $12 per trade. Free real-time quotes with an account. Also offers mutual funds. $5000 minimum account balance.

- **J.B. Oxford** – *http://www.jboxford.com*. Commissions start at $14.50 per trade. Unlimited real time quotes. Also offers mutual funds, bonds, and options trading. $2000 minimum account balance. Customers receive free internet access as long as they keep the minimum balance in the account.
- **Killiney Investments** – *http://www.fin-trade.com*. A brokerage company which offers internet based dealing service in FX, futures, options, and stocks for both institutional and private investors.
- **InternetTrading** – *http://www.internettrading.com*
- **LiveTrade.com** – *http://www.livetrade.com*. Live Level 2 screens, execution via all ECNs, NYSE, and portfolio management.
- **LowTrades.com** – *http://www.lowtrades.com*. This online broker offers limit orders and market orders for $4 per trade. Do your research with InvestorGuide Research (*http://investorguide.com/researChâteauhtm*) and place cheap orders here.
- **Market Touch Web** – *http://www.bsdmtweb.com*. $15 per trade under 1000 shares.
- **MB Trading** – *http://www.mbtrading.com*. Day trading. $15 to $24 per trade.
- **Muriel Siebert & Co.** – *http://www.msiebert.com*. $15 per trade.
- **Mr. Stock** – *http://www.mrstock.com*. $15 per trade up to 1000 shares. Also offers mutual funds and options.
- **Mydiscountbroker.com** – *http://www.mydiscountbroker.com*. $12 per trade up to 5000 shares.
- **National Discount Brokers** – *http://www.ndb.com*. $14.75 per trade for market orders, $19.75 per trade for limit orders. Real time quotes. Over 7500 mutual funds. $2000 minimum account balance.
- **Net-Invest** – *http://www.net-invest.com*. From Capital International Securities Group. $25 per trade. Also in Spanish.
- **NetVest** – *http://www.netvest.com*. Discount Broker.
- **NobleTrading** – *http://www.nobletrading.com*. Online direct access brokerage firm offering choice of per share and per trade commission schedules. Trade using RealTick, E-Signal with order entry, The Shield, and the NobleTrader Level 2. Commission schedule ranges from $9.95 to $14.95, or 1.5 cents to one cent per share.
- **Norwest** – *http://www.norwest.com*.
- **Peremel Online** – *http://www.peremel.com*.
- **Quick and Reilly** – *http://www.quick-reilly.com*. $15 per trade for market orders, or $20 for limit orders. Also offers options trading. No minimum account balance. Two ways to trade, including one with the aid of a broker.
- **Regal** – *http://www.eregal.com*. $20 for NASDAQ trades of 1000 or more shares, $25 below 1000 shares, and $29 for listed trades up to 5000 shares. Unlimited real time quotes. No minimum account balance. Every tenth trade is free. Margin rate is 0.5% above the brokerage call rate.
- **R. J. Thompson Securities** – *http://www.rjt.com/default.html*

- **RML Trading** – *http://www.rmltrading.com.*
- **RushTrade.com** – *http://www.rushtrade.com.*
- **Sanford Securities** – *http://www.sanford.com.au.* Australia.
- **Schwab** – *http://www.schwab.com.* Allows you to buy and sell stocks, mutual funds, options, and treasuries. $30 trades up to 1000 shares, or 3 cents a share for more than 1000 shares. They also offer 50 real-time quotes per trade, plus research from Credit Suisse First Boston and Hambrecht and Quist for $30 per month. $5000 minimum account balance.
- **ScoTTrade** – *http://www.scottrade.com.* $7 per trade for market orders, $12 per trade for limit orders. 100 real time quotes per trade. $2,000 account minimum. Also options trading.
- **ShareBuilder** – *http://www.sharebuilder.com.* Buy and sell stocks in dollar amounts. No account or investment minimums. Only $2 per transaction.
- **Sharex.com** – *http://www.sharex.com.*
- **Sherry Bruce's State Discount Brokers** – *http://www.state-discount.com.*
- **Sloan Securities** – *http://www.sloansecurities.com.*
- **SuccessTrade.com** – *http://www.successtrade.com.* For daytraders - $7.95 per trade for market and limit orders.
- **Summit Trading** – *http://www.summittrading.com.* Day trading. Downloadable software.
- **SpeedTrader** – *http://www.speedtrader.com.* $15 to $20 per trade.
- **Stockwalk.com** – *http://www.stockwalk.com.* Trade bonds and CDs, too.
- **SuccessTrade** – *http://www.successtrade.com.* All Trades only $9.95 a trade-includes market and limit orders.
- **Sunlogic** – *http://www.sunlogic.com.* $16 per trade.
- **Tradefast** – *https://www.tradeoptions.com.* 3 cents per share, $20 minimum.
- **Trade4Less** – *http://www.trade4less.com.*
- **TradeScape.com** – *http://www.tradescape.com.* Geared toward active traders. $1.50 per 100 shares, free Level II quotes, Direct ECN connections. Educational products.
- **TradeSecurities.com** – *http://www.tradesecurities.com.* After-hours trading. $25,000 minimum account balance. Commissions of 6 cents per share, minimum $100.
- **TradeWallStreet.com** – *http://www.tradewallstreet.com.* Full service broker providing direct access trading from $9.95 per trade.
- **TradeWell** – *http://www.trade-well.com.*
- **Trading Direct** – *http://www.tradingdirect.com.* From York Securities. Commissions start at $10 per trade. Also offers options and mutual funds. No minimum account balance.
- **Trend Trader** – *http://www.trendtrader.com.* Day trading. Starts at $15 per trade.

- **T. Royou Price** – *http://www.troweprice.com/brokerage/index.html*. $25 per trade up to 1000 shares.
- **TruTrade** – *http://www.trutrade.com*. $11 per trade for OTC or less than 2000 shares of listed stocks. No-fee IRA, free checkwriting, mutual funds, and low margin rates.
- **USRica.com** – *http://www.usrica.com*. Trades executed for only $4.95 per trade, plus $2.50 service charge. Free unlimited real-time quotes, online account balance.
- **Vision Trade** – *http://www.visiontrade.com*. $15 per stock trade. Also offers options and mutual funds.
- **Wachovia** – *http://www.wachovia.com*.
- **WR Hambrecht** – *http://www.wrhambrecht.com*. Online broker offering $20 internet and $25 broker-assisted trades
- **Wall Street Access** – *http://www.wsaccess.com*. They focus on the active trader. Commissions start at $25 per trade. 100 free real-time quotes with each trade. Also offers Treasuries and options trading.
- **Wall Street Discount** – *http://www.wsdc.com*. Starts at $20 per trade.
- **Wall Street Electronica** – *http://www.wallstreete.com*. From Winston Rodgers & Otalvaro, a full-service firm. Commissions start at $15 per trade. Also offers bonds and options. $10,000 minimum account balance.
- **Wang** – *http://www.wangvest.com*. Commissions start at $5 per trade. Text is in Chinese or English.
- **Waterhouse webBroker** – *http://www.waterhouse.com*. $12 per trade up to 5,000 shares. Free real-time quotes, charts, news, S&P reports, and Zacks earnings estimates. Also offers mutual funds. 24-hour access to a live broker.
- **Web Street Securities** – *http://www.webstreetsecurities.com*. $15 per trade. NASDAQ trades of 1000 or more shares are commission-free. Ten second executions and one minute email confirmations. Streaming real-time portfolio management. Java-based interface.
- **WellsTrade** – *http://wellsfargo.com/wellstrade*. From Wells Fargo. $30 per trade.
- **White Discount Securities Online** – *http://www.wdsonline.com*.
- **Wit Capital** – *http://www.witcapital.com*. Stocks, mutual funds, and options.
- **Wyse** – *http://www.wyse-sec.com*. Starts at $8 per trade.
- **Your Discount Broker** – *http://www.ydb.com*. Day traders can pay $30 to trade in and out of any stock for a full day.

Appendix 2

Chart Personalities/Trends

I believe in personalities, cycles, patterns, complex mathematical models, and elasticity, when it comes to stock. By personalities, I am referring only to a stock's chart trend. There are many personalities; some are more complex. Just as we have many individuals in our families and in society, each with a slightly different personality, so is each stock chart like a picture of an individual personality.

By observing the past behaviour of a stock, it is possible to understand its limits, restrictions, strengths, and weaknesses. A good understanding of these factors in a stock's personality will give you confidence in prediction, when you are trading it. You will know the highs the stock is unlikely to exceed, and the lows it is unlikely to break, as well as how long a bullish or bearish trend will last.

Listed below and expanded on in this appendix, are a few basic stock personalities:

1. The Good Man (aka Upward Trending)
2. The Bad Man (aka Downward Trending)
3. The Yoyo (aka Repeating Pattern)
4. The Flyer
5. The Over Comer (aka The Consolidator)
6. The Post IPO Disaster

In the Stock Screener section on page 75, we shall look at how to find these basic personalities and some others that are more complex.

The Good Man (aka Upward Trending)

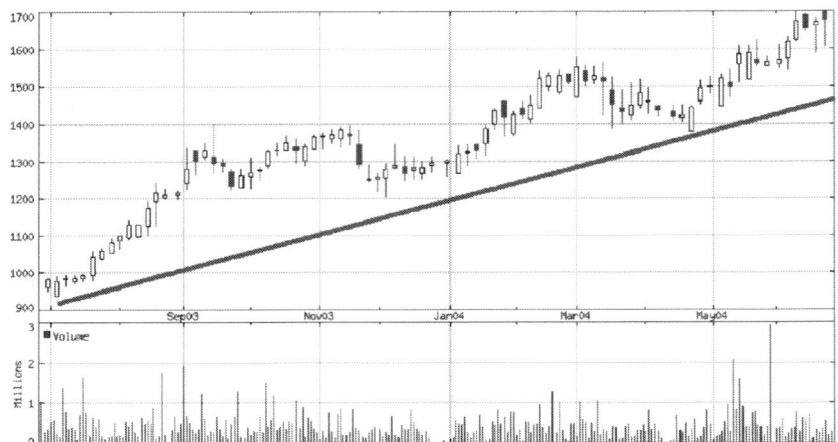

Figure 6: The Good Man (aka Upward Trending)

The Bad Man (aka Downward Trending)

Figure 7: The Bad Man (aka Downward Trending)

As already mentioned, stock personalities are just like human personalities in so many ways. Just as there are totally insane and unpredictable people out there, there are also totally unpredictable and random stocks out there. It is not your job to be able to predict the behaviour of every stock. To make a considerable amount of money, you only need to identify the extreme personalities. That is, the extremely stable and sound, and the extremely unstable and weak, in fundamental support.

The Yoyo (aka Repeating Pattern)

Figure 8: The Yoyo (aka Repeating Pattern)

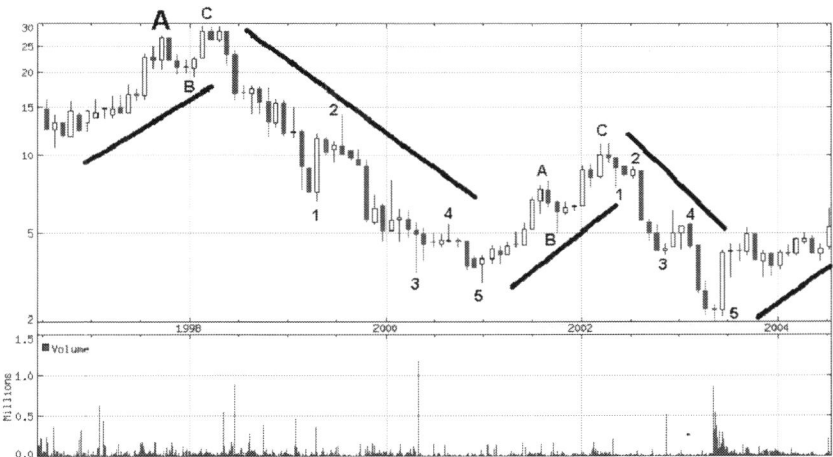

Figure 9: Another Yoyo

The myriad of stock whose personalities fall between these two extremes will be prone to switching between stable behaviour and unstable behaviour. Amongst these will be those whose behaviour follows a pattern, a predictable cycle of ups and downs, very much like a recovering alcoholic or a person who goes from relationship to relationship making the same mistakes, which lead to a break-up or divorce. See Figure 8 and Figure 9.

The Flyer

Figure 10: The Flyer

In addition, amongst these will be stock that have a crisis or life changing event occur, causing them to change personality. This could be compared with the behaviour of an irresponsible bachelor who settles down and has a child, causing him to become stable, responsible, and reliable. The inverse could also happen. A married individual, who was reliable, stable, and responsible to his partner and family, suddenly discovers that his partner is seeing someone else, and has been for many years. The divorce and shock arising from this may cause the individual to become a loose cannon, never trusting a stable relationship again.

The Over Comer (aka The Consolidator)

Figure 11: The Over Comer (aka the Consolidator)

The Consolidator personality occurs when a stock is rapidly heading in one direction (generally down). It stops, stabilises at new price level for a period of time, and then attempts to break out of the price range once it has built up enough strength to move on. This personality can be likened to a recovering alcoholic, whose life is rapidly degenerating. The loss of their home, partner, and job, may have sunk them to new lows. From these new lows, with help and support, our ex-alcoholic begins to rebuild their life, and eventually return to the previous highs they enjoyed.

Alternatively, they may become disillusioned and loose confidence and energy, never to recover, and spiral into lower depths.

The Post IPO Disaster

Figure 12: IPO

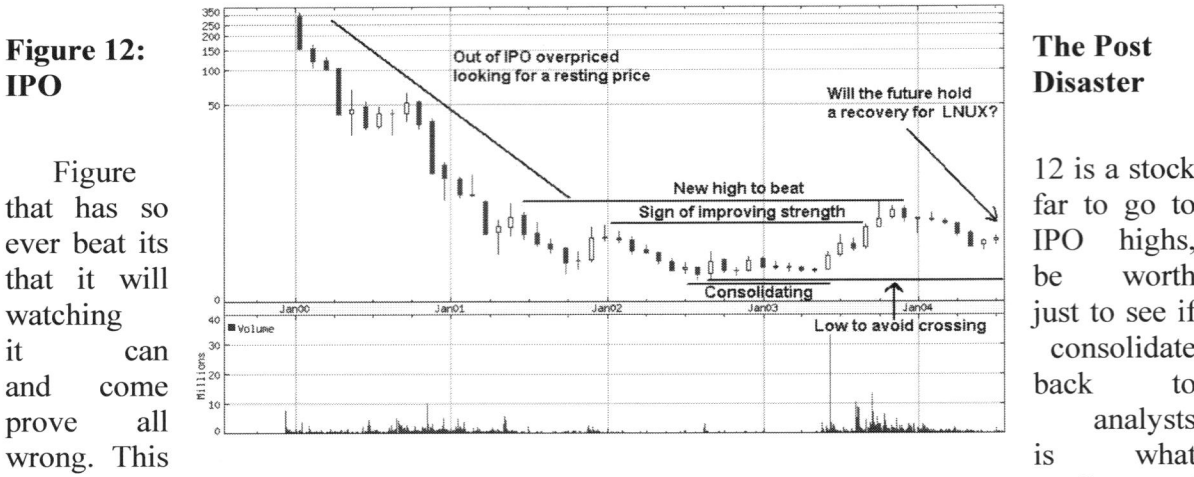

The Post Disaster

Figure that has so ever beat its that it will watching it can and come prove all wrong. This

12 is a stock far to go to IPO highs, be worth just to see if consolidate back to analysts is what

happens when too much excitement precedes a launch. Valuations can become totally out of synch with reality. Avoid this personality and stock for gains on the upside, during the initial fervour. After the excitement when the prices start falling to where they really belong, you can profit handsomely with shorting techniques that I will cover later.

As you can see, there are as many personalities as there are people, and likewise there are as many stock personalities as there are stocks.

There are numerous tools available to aid you in understanding stock personalities. These tools are called indicators. Next, I will cover the indicators that I find most useful for the techniques that I use to trade.

Chart Attributes

Before we begin, let me give you a quick grounding in charting knowledge. A stock chart is a graphical representation of a stock's historical price movement. There are many things that a chart can show, and any chart's usefulness is normally dependent on the way and method that it is viewed.

The first thing that you will need to know about charts is the range displayed. All chart ranges tell a different story about a stock's price movement. Let us see General Electric (GE) viewed over different time frames.

Time Frames

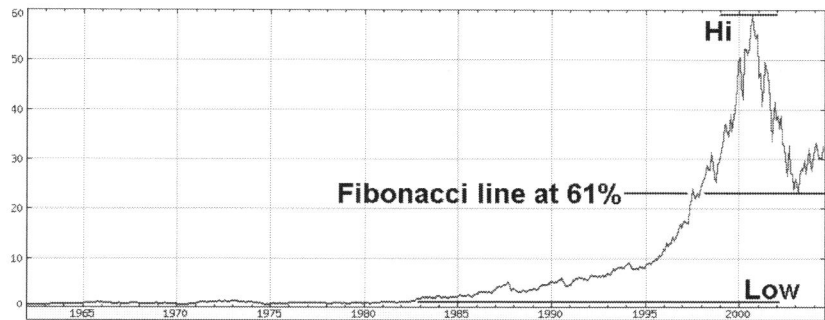

Figure 13: GE since floating

In this view (Figure 13), it seems like GE was doing nothing until early 1980 when it started to grow rapidly to its peak around the last quarter of 2000. It then lost its value to the Fibonacci 61.8% line. The equation to calculate this bounce is as follows:

$$Hi - ((Hi\text{-}Low) \times 0.618)$$

$$59 - ((59\text{-}1) * 0.618) = \$23.156$$

More will be covered on Fibonacci later.

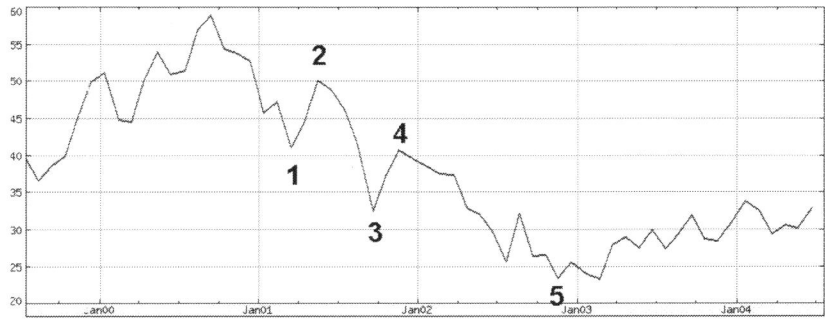

Figure 14: GE over 5 years

In the 5-year view (Figure 14), it seems that GE is very bearish, as the Elliot Wave analysis indicates. More will be covered on the Elliot Wave analysis later.

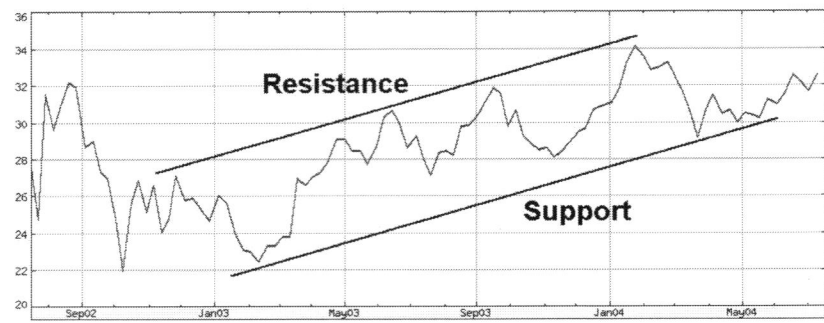

Figure 15: GE over 2 years

In the 2-year view (Figure 15), you can see that there is a channel developing by drawing a support and a resistance line. For the channel to hold its integrity, the support and resistance must not be crossed. If they were breached, it would signal a personality change within this view.

Figure 16: GE over 12 months

The 12-month view in Figure 16 highlights the tail end of the channel from Figure 15.

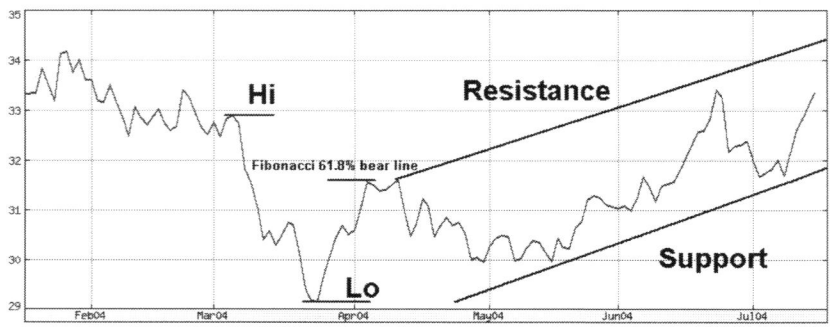

Figure 17: GE over 6 months

From the 6-month chart in Figure 17, you see a bounce on the downside to the Fibonacci 61.8% line, 31.51 = (29.25 + ((32.9 − 29.25) * 0.618)). You can also see a short-term channel developing.

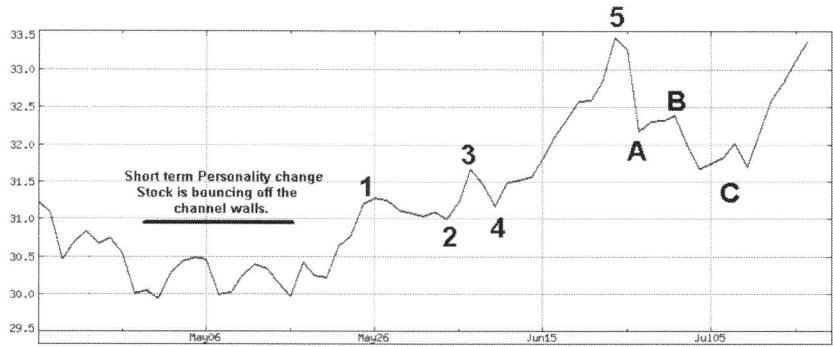

Figure 18: GE over 3 months

If you look back to the 6-month chart (Figure 17), you will see that the 3-month chart is displaying a short-term personality change as it reverses direction within the channel indicated in the 6-month chart. You can see with Elliot Wave Analysis that you are moving for another climb to the resistance line.

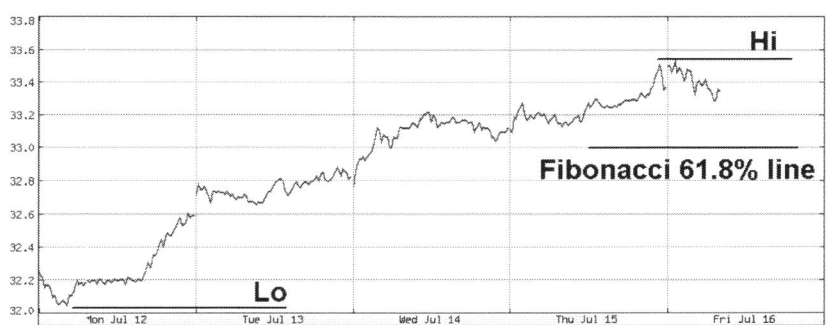

Figure 19: GE over 5 days

You can see from the 5-day chart in Figure 19, that the stock is headed for a bounce off the Fibonacci 61.8% line at $33.88 = ((34.5 − ((34.5 - 32.07) x 0.618)). Therefore, if you were trading this stock daily, you would know to get back in around $33.

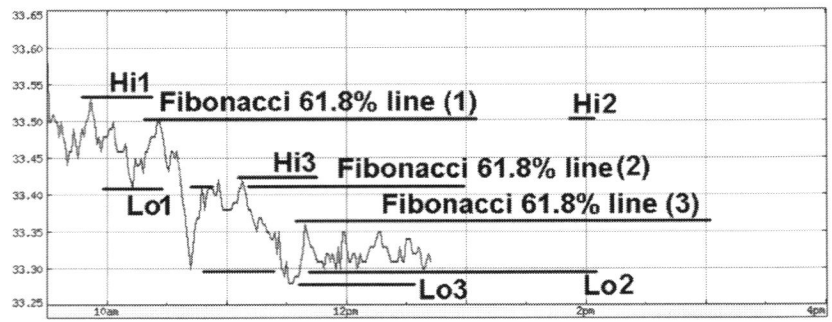

Figure 20: GE over part of a day

From viewing this stock from over 5 years all the way to one day (Figure 20), you will now know that this stock will fall to around $33. You can also see that you can use Fibonacci to trade this stock as a day trader. Here are the Fibonacci calculations:

- Fibonacci 61.8% line (1) = 33.42 + ((33.54 – 33.42) x 0.618) = $33.49
- Fibonacci 61.8% line (2) = 33.3 + ((33.49 - 33.3) x 0.618) = $33.42
- Fibonacci 61.8% line (3) = 33.28 – ((33.425 – 33.28) x 0.618) = $33.37

Always know where you are at any time in a stock; step back to its full history, then review a stock's whole history, 10-year, 5-year, 2-year, 12-months, 6-month, 3-months, 1-month, 5-day, and 1-day chart. If you are buying more long-term, only review down to 12 months. If your are trading medium-term i.e. holding a stock for a month to 3 months, then only review down to 1-month view charts.

This technique is fantastic as you have seen, but let us improve on it a little more. So far, you have only looked at line charts. Next, you look at the other chart types.

Chart Types

We have covered time frames and how to use them. The chart type you use to view a stocks price movement will determine the accuracy of entry and exit of your trades. There are over five stock chart types. There are five of them, listed as follows:

Mountain chart

The mountain chart as it is called, looks like mountains against a light sky. It is a line chart with the area under the price line filled in a darker colour, as in Figure 21. I do not use this chart because it is useless for trading. However, it is excellent for general price representations in reports.

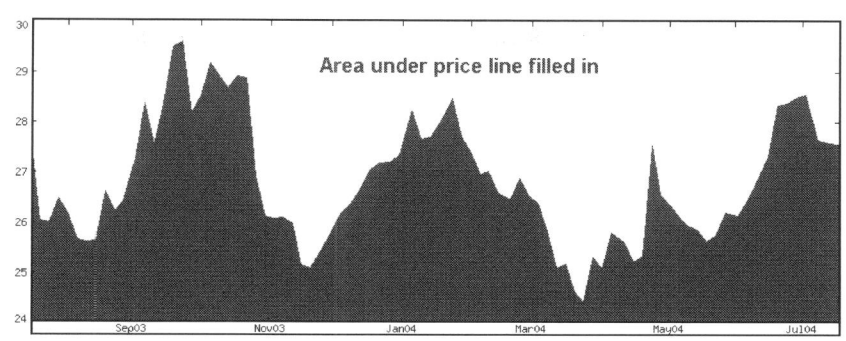

Figure 21: The Mountain chart

Line chart

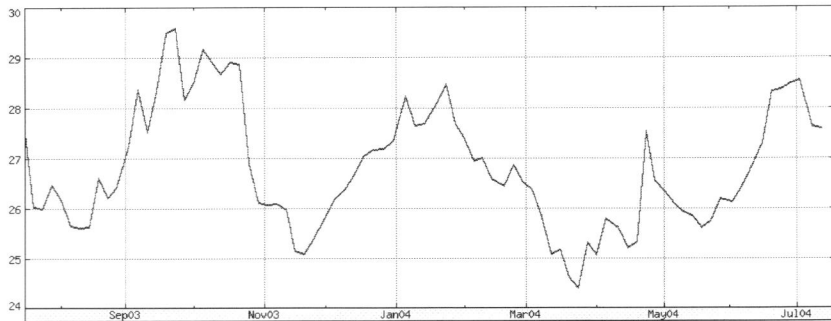

Figure 22: The Line chart

As the name suggests, this chart type uses a single line to represent price movement. It averages off spikes, thus it is not a very accurate representation of daily price swings. However, it is better than the Mountain chart.

Open high low close (OHLC) chart

Figure 23: OHLC Chart

The OHLC chart type gives you the lowest price of the period and the highest price of the period, as well as the open and close prices. They are useful for analysing stock charts; however, I never use them because they lack something extra, an immediate visual indication of trend. You will see this problem resolved in the candlestick charts.

There is a variation of the OHLC chart, which is similar to the OHLC except it does not show the open prices, and is called the HLC chart.

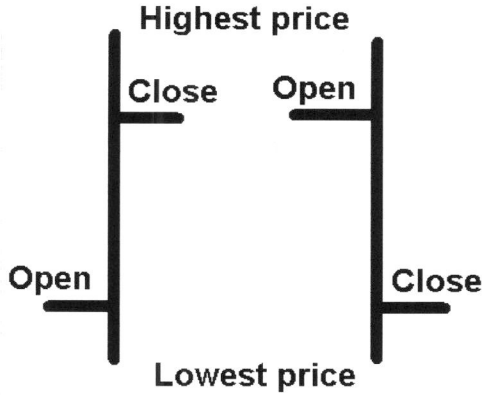

Figure 24: OHLC chart price indicators

Dot chart

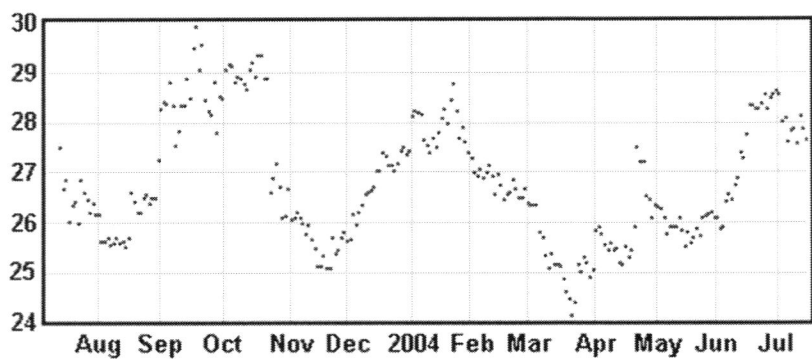

Figure 25: The Dot Chart

This chart (Figure 25) uses single dots to represent the average price of the session (i.e. a day). As you can see, it is not the easiest to read. It is better than Mountain or Line charts for accuracy, although it cannot beat OHLC for information.

Candlestick chart

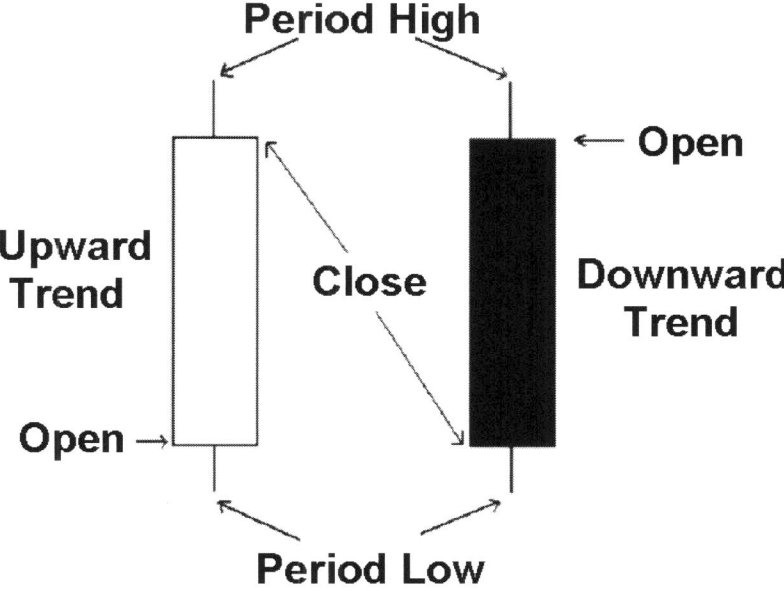

Figure 26: The candlestick

Figure 27: The candlestick chart

Now you come to my personal favourite chart, the candlestick chart. This is by far the best chart type for the serious trader. There are two candlesticks, the light coloured one (normally white), and the darker candlestick (normally black or blue). As you can see in Figure 26, the candlestick at any moment represents the following:

1. The period high
2. The period low

3. The period trend
4. The open price
5. The close price
6. The periods open and close spread
7. The period's open to high spread
8. The period's open to close spread
9. The period's close to high spread
10. The period's close to low spread

This is why I love the candlestick chart so much. You get so much information just with one glance. The candlestick chart is a great trigger of stock personality changes. Let us now use it to analyse Microsoft (MSFT) in the following charts.

Using candlesticks to analyse stock

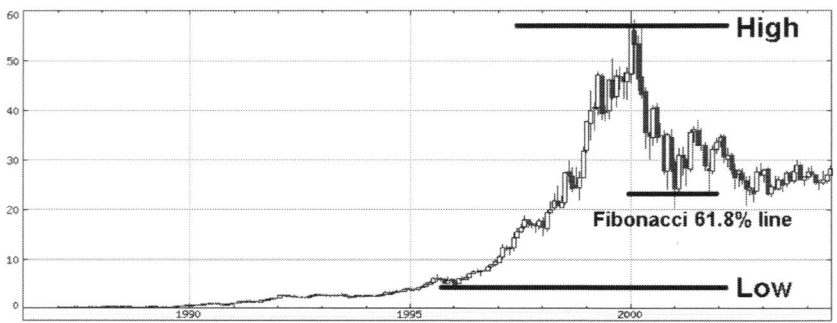

Figure 28: Candlestick chart of MSFT since floating

Before you can correctly analyse the 12-month chart, you will need to take a look at the full chart history of MSFT. You can see that the market conditions that affected GE (displayed previously) also affected MSFT. Let us take a closer look at how MSFT reacted. From Figure 28, you can see that MSFT bounced off the Fibonacci 61.8% line. The calculation of this is as follows:

Fibonacci 61.8% line = 57- ((57-4.5) x 0.618) = $24.553

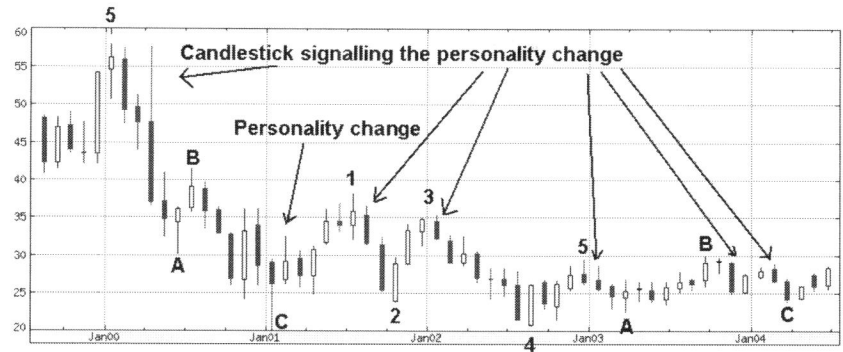

Figure 29: 5-year Candlestick chart of MSFT

From MSFT's 5-year chart, you can see that this company is quite strong in fundamentals. How? Well, it bounced off the Fibonacci 61.8% line in Jan 2001, and then very quickly dissipated the downward momentum. Note that it never went below the Jan 2001 low. It has been consolidating since August 2002. Now it looks as though it is about to break out of the C of April 2004. The first target it will rise to claim is around the $30 mark. Once it has successfully crossed $30, it will head for $35, $37.50, $42.50, and finally the big one $57.50.

You cannot tell how fast this will happen, but you know that if MSFT breaks out of $30, it will not stop. This is because it has dissipated its downward momentum from the Jan 2000, it has not been back across the Jan 2001 lows since Jan 2001, and it has been testing the $30 mark several times now (Dec 2002 and Sep 2003). The next time it tests the $30 resistance line may be the breaking point.

Figure 30: 6-month MSFT chart attempting to drill out of the long-term channel

If you wanted to trade MSFT short-term, you will need to analyse the shorter period charts as well as the longer term charts. As you can see in the 6-month chart of Figure 30, candlesticks can give us more information than the other chart types. Note that there are mixtures of white and black candlesticks on the price falls, and mainly white ones on price increases. This tells you that the stock is bullish. It is resisting going down but not up. That is one of the reasons why it will be able to break the $30 barrier soon.

In Figure 30, you will also notice that there are two channels, a long-term channel, and a short-term channel. The direction of a stock's channel tells you the direction of its trend. This is because to channel, a stock has to test highs and lows, frequently breaking new levels as the stock develops momentum and strength, whether up or down.

Note that in Figure 30, on the downside from Jan 2004 to late March 2004, it moved to the support of the long-term channel. To facilitate an attempted long-term resistance channel breach, it used a smaller channel within the long-term channel, to build power, strength, and momentum. The walls of the long-term channel are stronger than the short-term channels, but with the aid of the short-term channel, MSFT can penetrate the long-term channel wall and escape to new highs.

As the long-term channel has not been breached yet, it would be an unnecessary risk to go long (buy the stock) right now. However, if the long-term channel is breached, and the stock price rises above $30, I would be very bullish on MSFT.

As you have seen, using the candlestick chart type allows you to extract stock personality information to help you time your entry into, and exit from trades.

Volume

Another indicator that gives you vital information about a stock is its volume. The volume or trading volume is the amount of shares sold in a period. The period is the time division represented by each candlestick. The volume indicates the following:

1. The stock's volatility. How quickly it can change directions or price.
2. The interest trend, if investors are buying more of the stock, or selling more of it in a set time frame. An example of this would be the inclusion of a stock in the S&P Index, which would cause the stock to show a sudden jump in volume to higher averages.
3. Sudden interest, a sharp rise in buying or selling. This is normally related to news.
4. The width of the market makers spread. This is the difference between the ask and the bid. Normally, the higher the volume, the thinner the spread; and the lower the volume, the wider the spread).

Figure 31: Volume signalling

When used in conjunction with the other indicators and chart types, the volume of a stock can indicate a change in personality, several time intervals before the actual change occurs. In Figure 31, the time interval is one day per volume bar. Therefore, in this case, volume signalling will provide you with two or more days advance warning of a personality change. Why is this possible? No one really knows exactly why this is, but I suspect it is due to early knowledge of upcoming news by institutional traders, and pertly to do with some insider trading.[4]

An indicator that is displayed in the same section of the chart as the volume is the Moving Average Convergence Divergence or MACD. Let us find out how we can use it.

Moving Average Convergence Divergence - MACD

Another good indicator is the Moving Average Convergence Divergence (MACD). It calculates the trend and momentum of stock by subtracting the 26-day Exponential Moving Average (EMA), which gives more weight to latest values from a 12-day EMA. A 9-day EMA of the MACD called the signal line, is then plotted on top of the MACD. If this sounds complex to you, it is much more comprehendible when viewed graphically.

As you can see from Figure 32, the stock chart with the 20-day MA and 50-day MA, are at the top of the chart. In the middle part of the chart lies the volume bars, and at the bottom of the chart we can see the MACD and signal line. The MACD is the chart with the bars evenly spread out. The MACD bars in this case also show divergence. They swing from positive, showing a bullish trend, to negative, showing a bearish trend. See Figure 33.

---

[4] Insider trading, is trading undertaken with knowledge of the internal situations of a company. It is normally illegal, and frowned on, but this does not stop it from occurring.

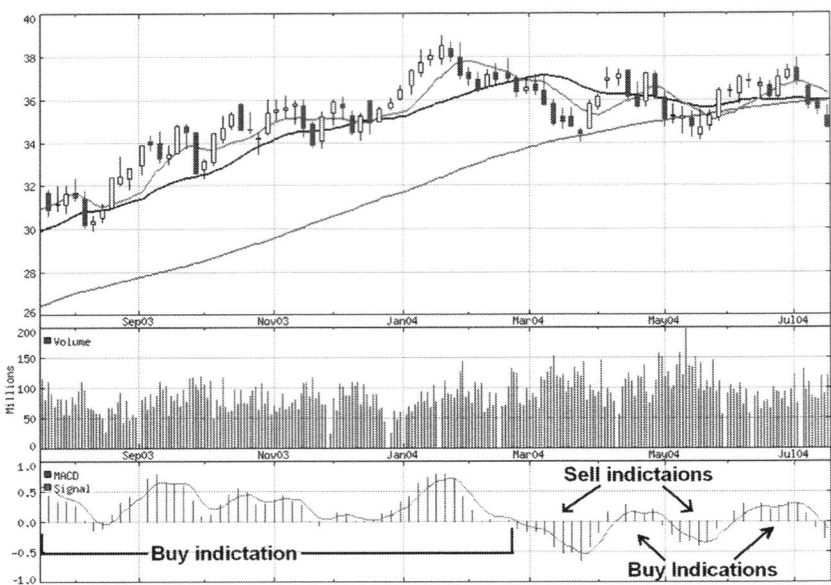

Figure 32: Chart with MAs, Volume, MACD, and signal line

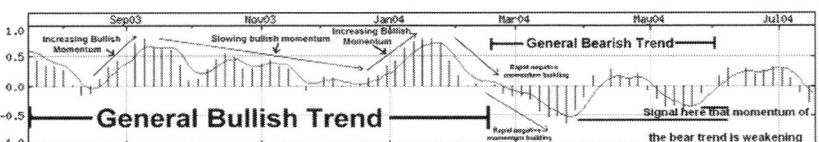

Figure 33: MACD and signal line

You can use the MACD to obtain the following:

1. When the MACD sits below the signal line, a buy signal is indicated (see Figure 32).
2. When the MACD sits above the signal line, a sell signal is indicated (see Figure 32).
3. When the signal line diverges from the MACD, this signals the end of a trend.
4. When the MACD rises quickly, it is a signal that the stock is over-bought, or over-sold in the case of the stock falling quickly. Shortly after these occurrences, the stock price soon returns to normal levels.

In Figure 33, we can see how the rate of rise or fall of the MACD indicates an elastic stretch of the stock to new local highs or lows. From the peaks of these +0.5 or greater (i.e. – 0.5 to -1, or 0.5 to 1) a price reversal normally occurs.

Note the weaker MACD signal in mid May 2004. This MACD peak was less than the end of Mar 2004 MACD peak, signalling a weakening of the bearish momentum.

For more information on moving averages, the MACD, and signal line, see *http://www.investopedia.com/terms/m/moving average.asp.*

Chart Patterns

There are many chart patterns available to you. We will now look at the main chart patterns.

Upward slope

When the last 5 highs have exceeded their previous highs, and the last 5 lows have not exceeded their last 5 lows, you will have an upward sloping chart (see Figure 34). Before trading this chart, look for strong and consistent volume as well as the MACD and signal line being mainly above the 0 line.

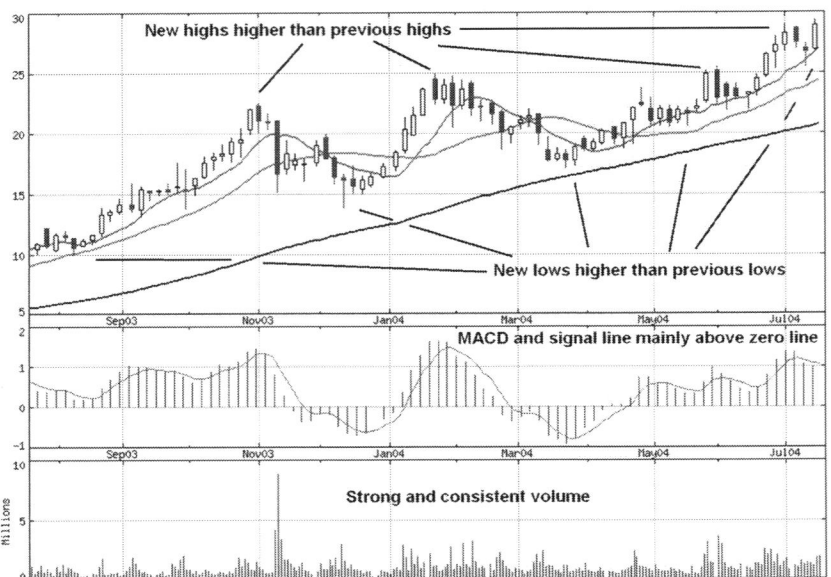

Figure 34: Upward slope chart

Downward slope

The reverse of the upward slope is the downward slope. This is a chart showing the last 5 lows exceeding the previous lows, and the last 5 highs have not exceeded their last 5 highs (see Figure 35). Before trading this chart, look for strong and consistent volume as well as the MACD and signal line being mainly below the 0 line.

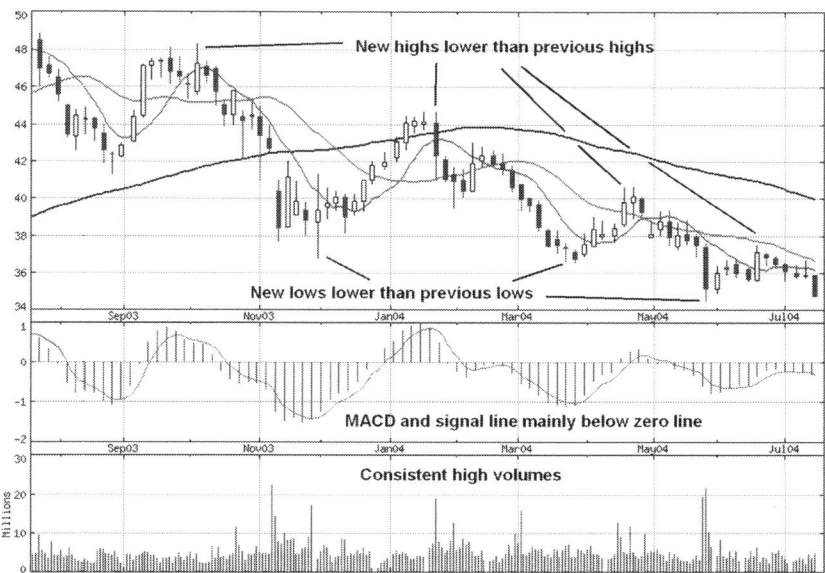

Figure 35: Downward slope chart

Head and shoulders

The head and shoulders chart pattern is a pattern that appears to be the outline of two shoulders on either side of a head (see Figure 36). It signals a change of personality away from the Head. Before trading this chart, look for strong and consistent volume, as well as the MACD and signal line rapidly crossing the 0 line. See MACD peak reversal in Figure 36. The sell short signal is the low price of the second shoulder. When this price is breached as it was in May 2004, you will have a completed head and shoulders pattern. Do not trade until you have a completed pattern.

The inverse head and shoulders is a reverse of this chart.

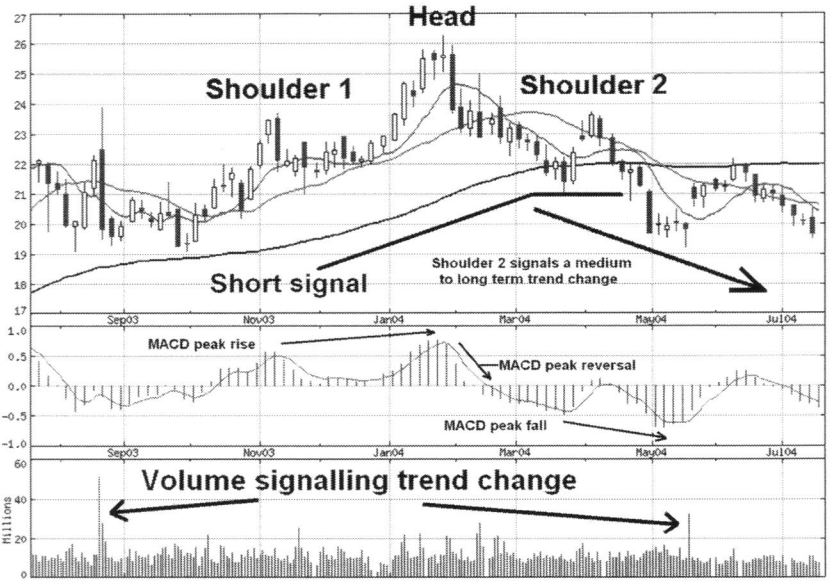

Figure 36: Head and Shoulders Chart

Bowl

The bowl chart pattern looks like an outline of a breakfast bowl. It is an indicator to the development of a long-term consolidation pattern, and exit from the bowl. In Figure 37 and Figure 38, you will see a bowl pattern with a failed exit. Sometimes if the stock is strong enough, it will successfully exit the bowl. The consolidation pattern immediately after the bowl exit attempt was a warning of the potential failure of the bowl exit (see Figure 37).

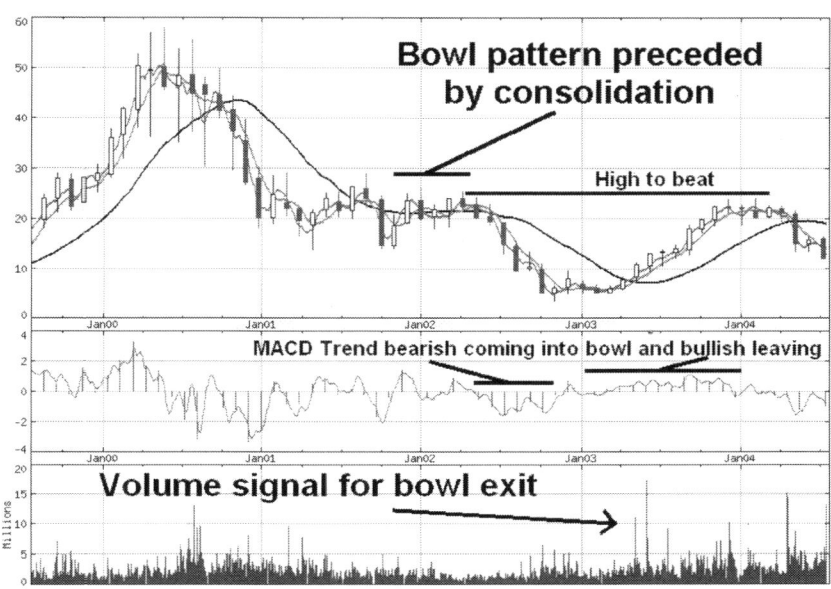

Figure 37: Bowl pattern 5-year view

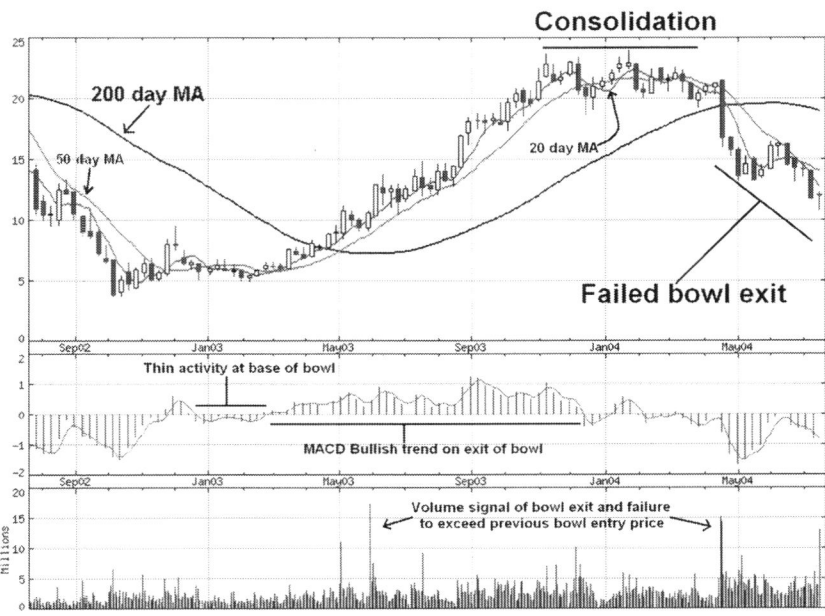

Figure 38: Bowl pattern 2-year view

This pattern can be traded short (selling short), if consolidation occurs before a total bowl exit. It can also be traded long if the pre-bowl entry consolidation prices are exceeded on the bowl exit (see Figure 38).

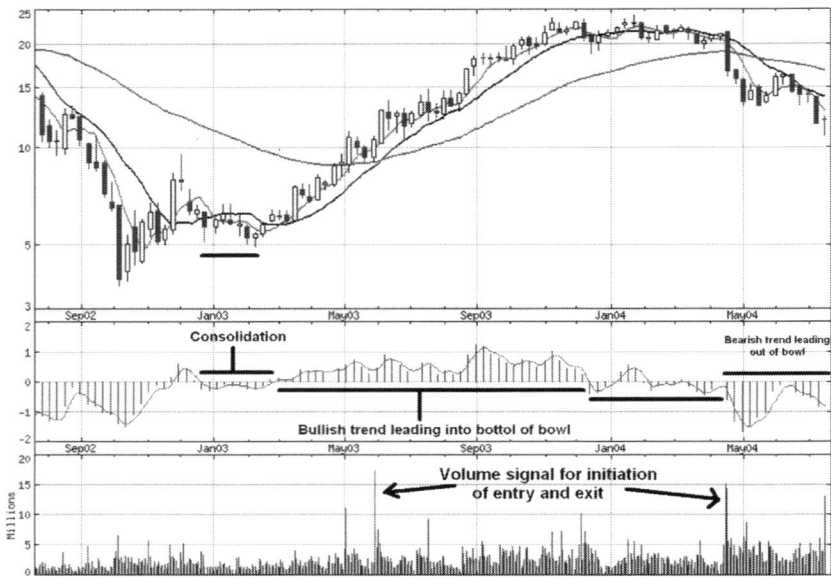

Figure 39: Inverse Bowl pattern

As you can see above, the same is true for the inverse bowl pattern. There is a small consolidation leading to the inverse bowl. The MACD and signal line are bullish during the inverse bowl entry. At the base of the bowl, the MACD thins out, and then reverses into a bearish trend until inverse bowl exit.

Cup and Handle

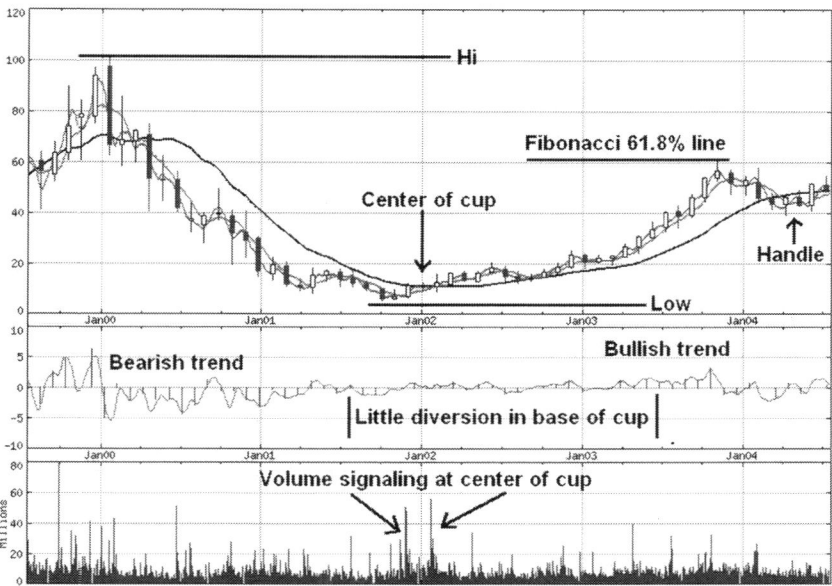

Figure 40: The Cup and Handle pattern

The cup and handle pattern is a failed bowl pattern. Like the bowl, it also occurs in reverse (inverse cup and handle). However, the cup and handle pattern does not normally start with consolidation, thus the failure to complete the bowl later on. It runs out of steam before reaching the previous high of the cup entry point. At this stage it begins consolidating, forming a handle.

The best way to trade the cup and handle pattern is to do as follows:

1. Take a short position at the Hi point (sell short).
2. Buy to close the stock when the MACD and signal line thin out in the centre of the cup.
3. Take a long position when the volume and/or MACD and the signal line start to increase in strength.
4. Set a stop limit order at the Fibonacci 61.8% line.

For the inverse cup and handle, trade as follows:

1. Take a long position at the Lo point (buy long).
2. Sell to close the stock when the MACD and signal line thin out in the centre of the cup.
3. Take a short (sell short) position when the volume and/or MACD and the signal line start to increase in strength.
4. Set a stop limit order at the Fibonacci 61.8% line.

M – for murder

Figure 41 Murder

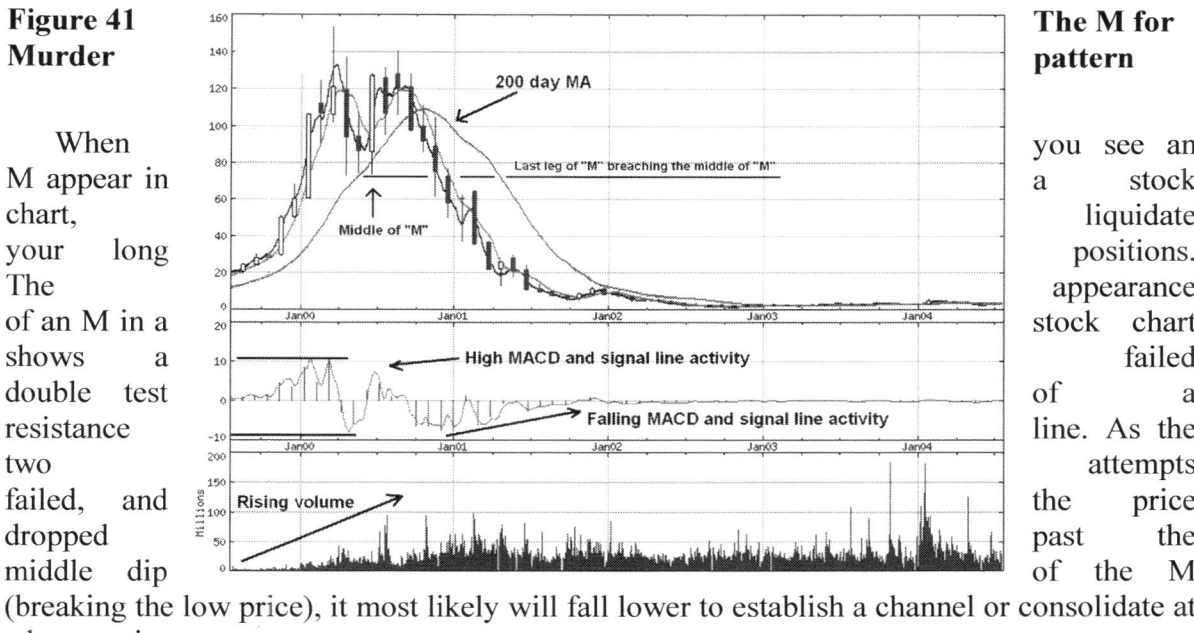

The M for pattern

When M appear in chart, your long The of an M in a shows a double test resistance two failed, and dropped middle dip (breaking the low price), it most likely will fall lower to establish a channel or consolidate at a lower price.

you see an a stock liquidate positions. appearance stock chart failed of a line. As the attempts the price past the of the M

To trade this pattern you will need to wait until the last leg of the M has been established. Take no action until the last leg has broken the last low price. Then and only then, should you short the stock (see Figure 41).

For the reverse of this, see the W – for winner pattern, next.

W – for winner

As with the M- for murder, the W signals a medium to long-term price reversal. A double attempt testing the bottom price and failing, signals a strong stock that is bullish. If this stock price then moves along the last leg of the W to break the middle of the W (the last high), it will most likely rapidly increase in price.

To trade this chart pattern you will need to wait until the last leg of the W has moved past the last high (middle of the W). Once this signal is established, you can go long on the stock (buy to open).

Elliot Wave

The way that the stock markets move is based on mass psychology. It was initially thought to be chaotic, and without any order. However, during 1929, Ralph Nelson Elliott discovered a repeating pattern in the stock markets. He found a fractal[5] type mathematical model to define the pullbacks and gains that a stock and the markets as a whole, go through.

---

[5] An object with a fractional dimension; one that has self-similar variations at all scales, in which the final level of detail is never reached, and never can be reached by increasing the scale at which observations are made.

This work was later improved on and published in the ground breaking book, *The Elliott Wave Principle – The Key to Stock Market Profits* by Robert Prechter and A.J. Frost (published by John Wiley and Sons Ltd). Acquire this book if you want to learn a lot more about this theory. I will be covering Elliot Wave theory at a basic level, so that anyone can understand it, and use it to create profits. You do not need t be a mathematician to do that.

The theory is simple enough; it states that there are five impulsive waves, and three corrective waves, in stock or market movement. If you looked closer at these waves you would see that smaller waves existed within each wave itself, and so on and so on, giving a fractal effect.

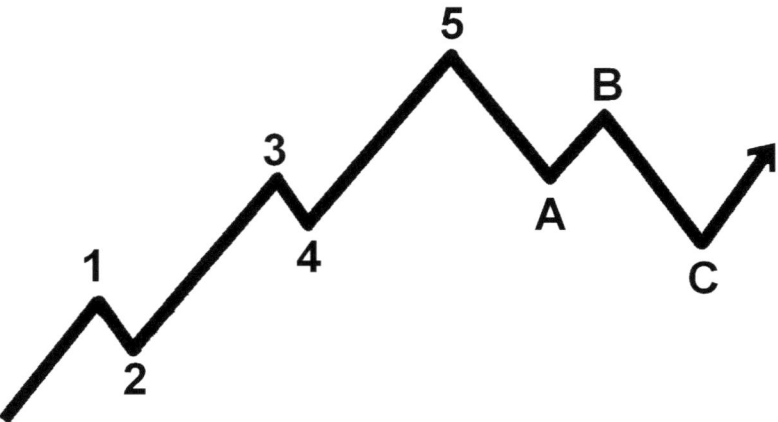

Figure 42: The basic principle of Elliot Wave theory

In Figure 42, you can see one cycle of the five impulsive waves, and three corrective waves. After C, the pattern will repeat itself starting back at 1 again.

Let us now have a look at some practical uses of this wave theory.

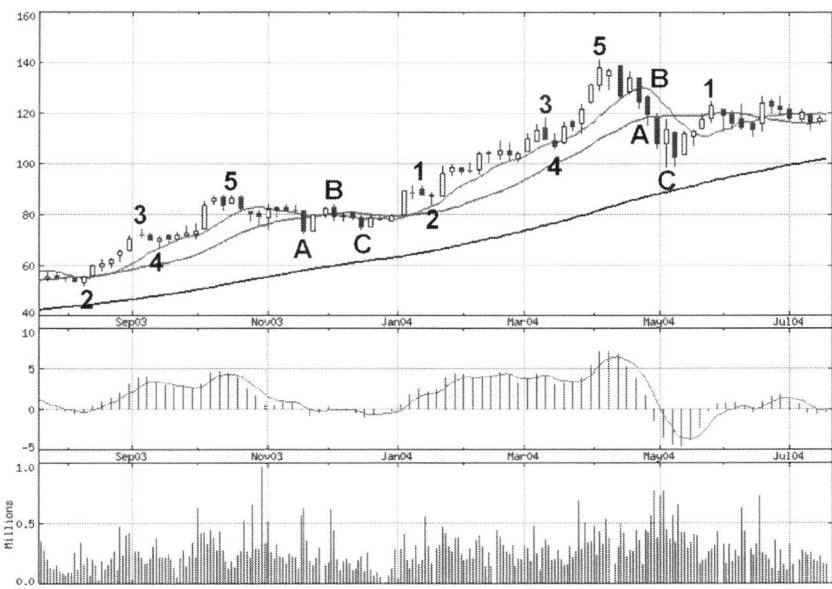

Figure 43: Elliot Wave analysis signalling

In the upward trending chart of Figure 43, you see that whenever the A, B, and C section of the chart is occurring, the MACD and signal line turn bearish.

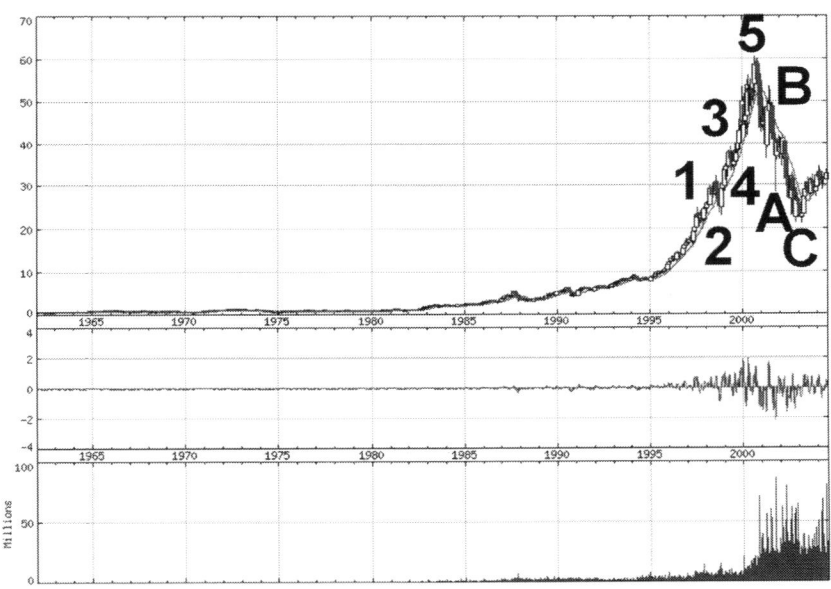

Figure 44: Elliot Wave analysis of GE over life of stock

In Figure 44, you see GE's stock over its lifetime. Because of price appreciation, long-term charts will always have more activity in their most recent times, than further back in their history.

Figure 45: Elliot Wave analysis of GE over 5 years

In Figure 45, you see GE coming off the highs of the last quarter of 2000. It is going through a personality change, from bullish trend to bearish.

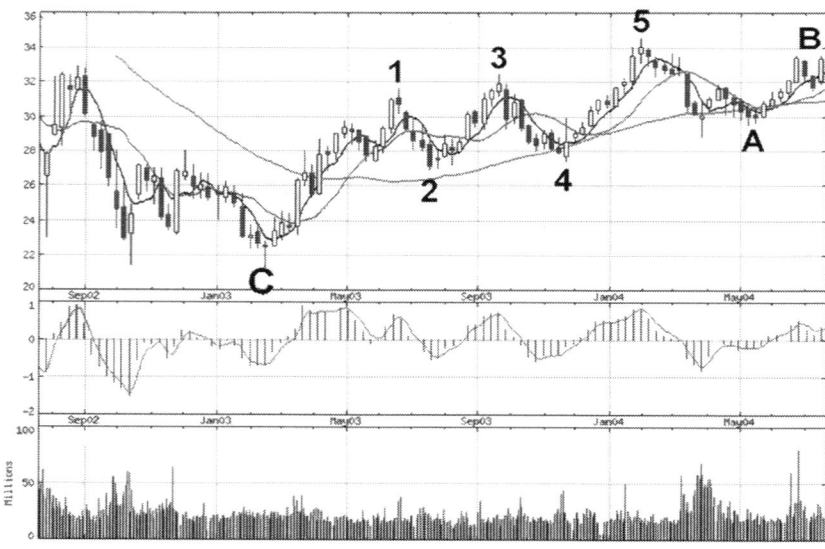

Figure 46: Elliot Wave analysis of GE over 2 years

Here in Figure 46, we have the end of the bearish trend. Now a steady bullish trend is building. Note the steady volume from Dec 2002 to March 2004.

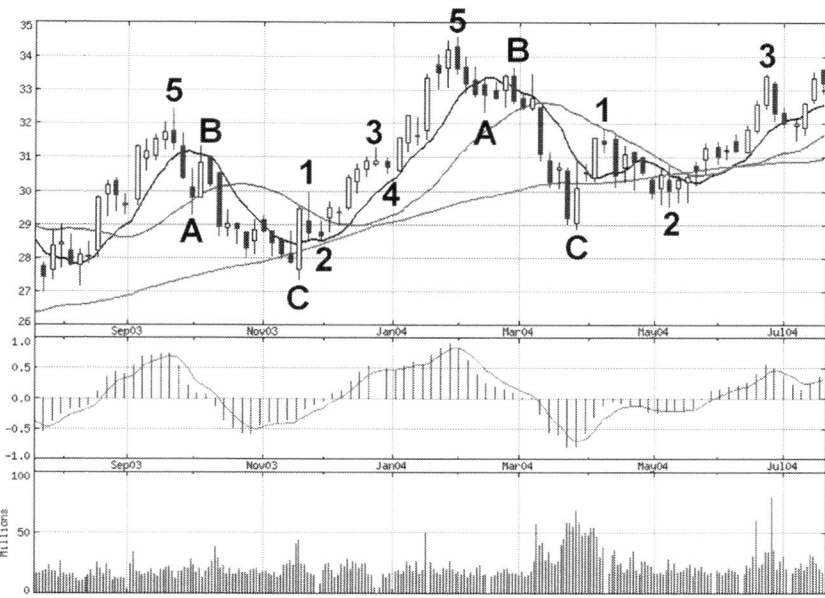

Figure 47: Elliot Wave analysis of GE over 12 months

Looking even closer, you see this fractal effect is still with us. The closer you get the view, the more you will see.

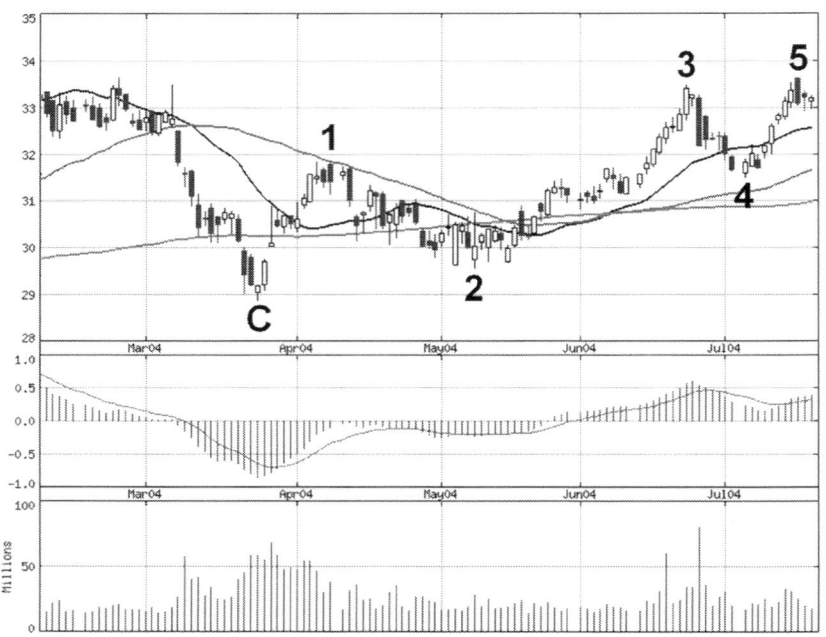

Figure 48 Elliot Wave analysis of GE over 6 months

The 5 at the far right hand side of Figure 48 shows a weakness in the bullish trend. You can see this because its price is almost the same as that of the 3. It may collapse during the next correction (A, B, and C). The moving averages have crossed (mid May 2004), and are trending upwards. This is a bullish sign, but will there be the strength?

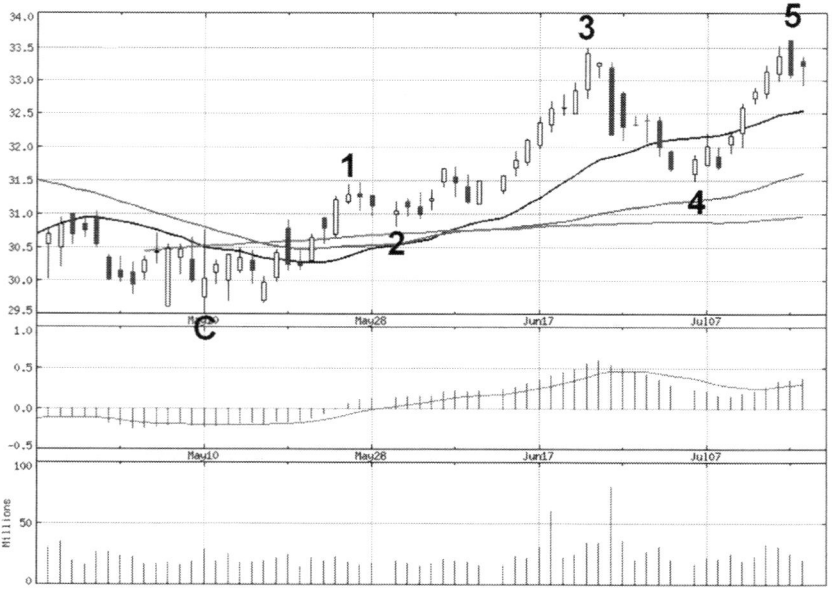

Figure 49: Elliot Wave analysis of GE over 3 months

At the end of this graph in Figure 49, we see the correction has begun.

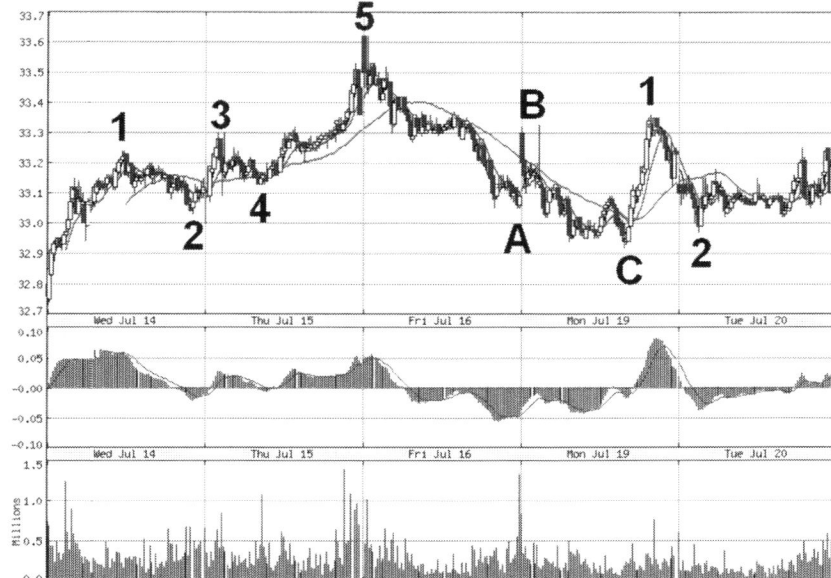

Figure 50: Elliot Wave analysis of GE over 10 days

In the 10-day chart, note the attempt to rise out of the weakness from C to 1. This attempt was short lived, and the return to 2 was sharp, highlighting the weakness even more.

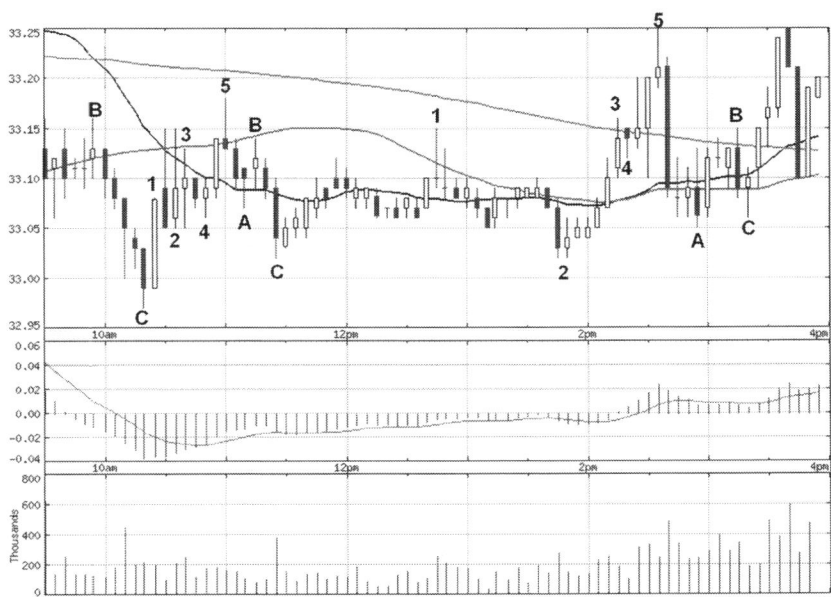

Figure 51: Elliot Wave analysis of GE over 1 day

In this one-day chart above, you see the fractal effect is still occurring. Each candlestick in this chart represents one minute with 20-minute, 50-minute, and 200-minute moving averages. The bullish trend is very weak, as you can see with MACD. Towards the end of the chart, the volume and MACD are showing signs of a rally.

There is nothing that beats preparedness when trading. Make sure you study only a few stocks at a time, and get to know their personalities. Doing this will reduce your chances of making a mistake due to an oversight or incorrect cycle prediction. Getting your Elliot Wave analysis skills honed will reduce trading risk and increase your profits.

Fibonacci

Fibonacci is the nickname of the 1170 AD born Algerian Educated Italian mathematician, Leonardo Pisano. For a full breakdown of Leonardo Pisano's achievements, go to *http:// www-groups.dcs.st-and.ac.uk/~history/Mathematicians/Fibonac ci.html*.

Leonardo Pisano produced several works of mathematical genius involving numbers. Leonardo Pisano's theory that you as an investor should be most interested in, is his number series theory.

Starting with the number 1, and using the sum of the current number and the previous number, you will get the following series:

1, 2, 3, 5, 8, 13, 21, 34, 55, etc

Carrying the series on will produce the following results:

1	0.000000000000000
2	0.500000000000000
3	0.666666666666667
5	0.600000000000000
8	0.625000000000000
13	0.615384615384615
21	0.619047619047619
34	0.617647058823529
55	0.618181818181818
89	0.617977528089888
144	0.618055555555556
233	0.618025751072961
377	0.618037135278515
610	0.618032786885246
987	0.618034447821682
1,597	0.618033813400125

2,584	0.618034055727554
4,181	0.618033963166707
6,765	0.618033998521803
10,946	0.618033985017358
17,711	0.618033990175597
28,657	0.618033988205325
46,368	0.618033988957902
75,025	0.618033988670443
121,393	0.618033988780243
196,418	0.618033988738303
317,811	0.618033988754323
514,229	0.618033988748204
832,040	0.618033988750541
1,346,269	0.618033988749648
2,178,309	0.618033988749989
3,524,578	0.618033988749859
5,702,887	0.618033988749909
9,227,465	0.618033988749890
14,930,352	0.618033988749897
24,157,817	0.618033988749894
39,088,169	0.618033988749895

If you then divide the last number by the current number, i.e. 1/2, 2/3, 3/5, 5/8, 8/13, etc, you will arrive at the constant, 0.618033988749895 (phi) eventually. This number can then be used to calculate a large array of naturally occurring phenomenon, like the stock market price bounces. For other applications of this theory, see *http://www.mcs.surrey.ac.uk/ Personal/R.Knott/Fibonacci/fibnat.html*.

So how can we use 0.618033988749895 (phi)? For stock trading, we can use it in many ways. The most exciting of these, is to predict bounces from the Elliot Wave analysis point 5 to point C.

The Fibonacci 61.8% line uses phi (0.618033988749895), as a percentage of the difference between the last 5, and the last C. This will give you the next C's bounce value.

By subtracting phi from 1, you get 0.381966011250105. This figure as a percentage will give you roughly 38.2%. This is the point A in Elliot Wave analysis. Therefore, the next A is calculated from 38.2% of the difference between the last 5 and C.

The equations for upward trend are:

Fibonacci 38.2% Line = Hi – ((Hi – Lo) x 0.381966011250105)

Fibonacci 61.8% Line = Hi – ((Hi – Lo) x 0.618033988749895)

In addition, the equations for downward trend are:

Fibonacci 38.2% Line = Lo + ((Hi − Lo) x 0.381966011250105)

Fibonacci 61.8% Line = Lo + ((Hi − Lo) x 0.618033988749895)

See the following charts in Figure 52, Figure 53, Figure 54, and Figure 55, which illustrate this theory.

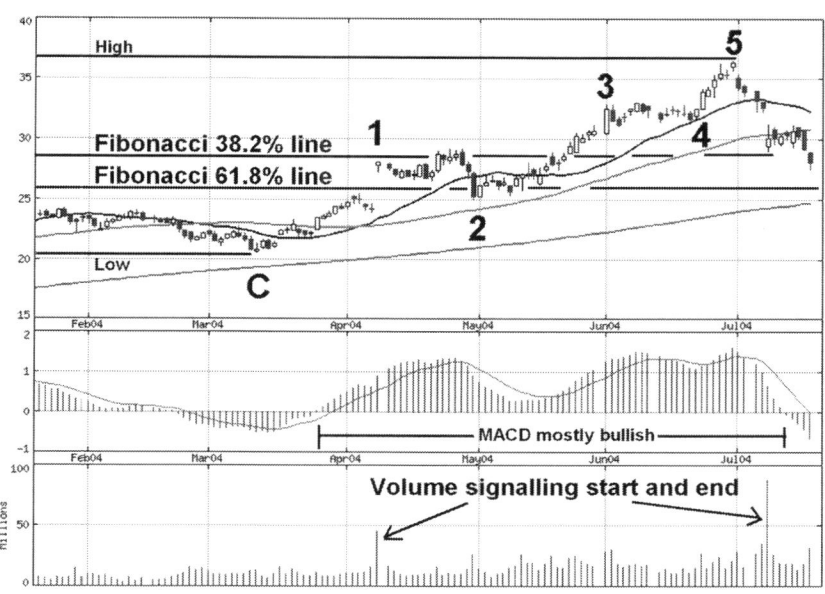

Figure 52: Fibonacci line bounced

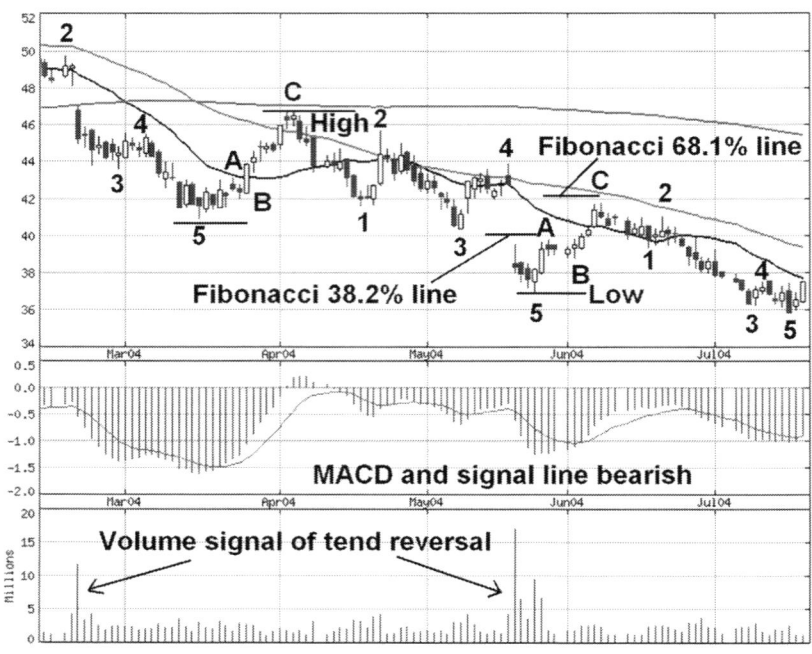

Figure 53: Fibonacci lines at A and C

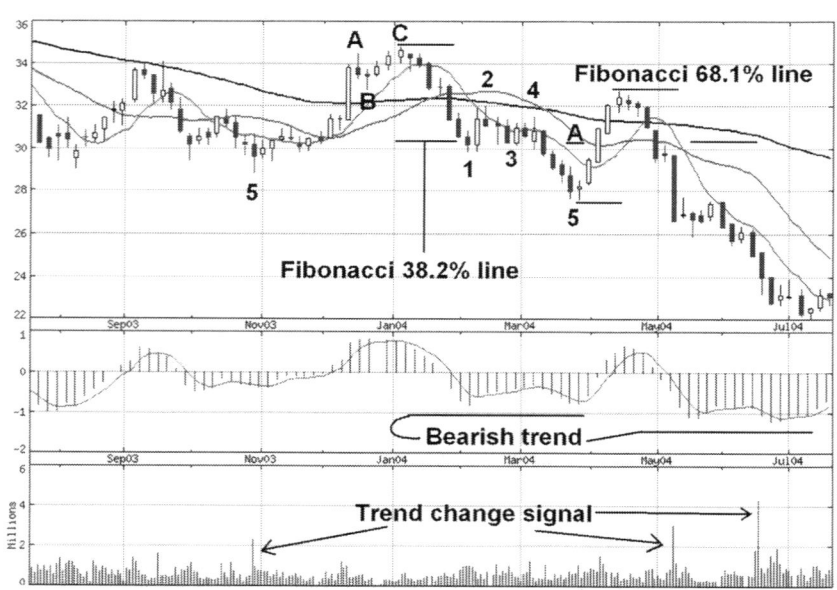

Figure 54: Fibonacci lines at A and C

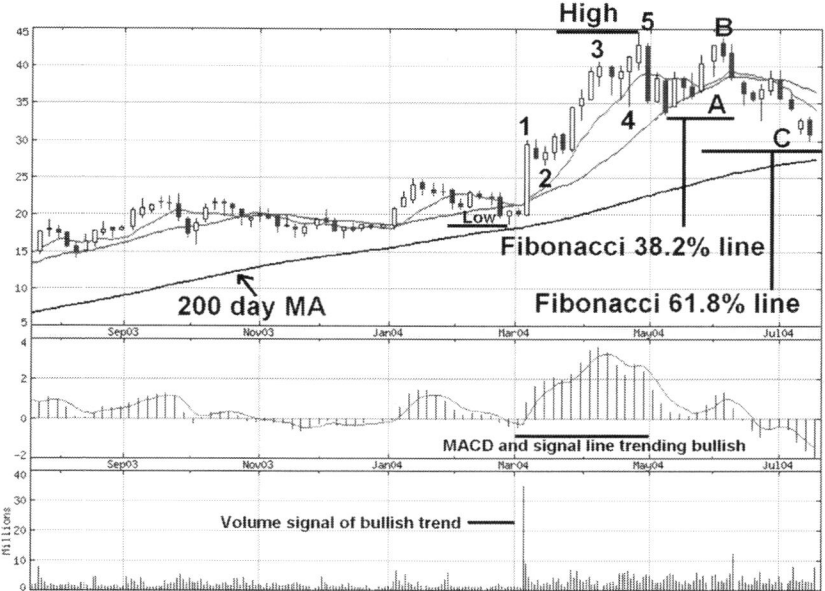

Figure 55: Fibonacci lines at A and C

So how do you trade this profitably? Whenever you see an Elliot Wave signal 5 on a stock chart, work out A and C using the Fibonacci 38.2% and 68.1% equations. You will know when the C will be, therefore allowing you to go long or short through the Elliot Wave signal 1, 2, 3, 4 and 5.

Other Factors

There are other factors to consider when trading in the stock markets: news. It is often the case that the news acts as a catalyst to energise or drain a stock of all its momentum and power (i.e. news on earnings or stock splits). To avoid getting into something that is reacting to a news item, always check the news background before your purchases.

Stock Selection Method

Let us now get more specific. There are thousands of stocks on any stock market. Selecting the ones with the personalities that you are interested in would be a long and tedious task if you had to sift through the charts manually one by one. To facilitate the automatic selection of stocks with desired personalities we will use a stock screener.

Stock Screeners

A stock screener is a tool for finding stock, given pre-supplied search criteria. There are hundreds of stock screeners available on the internet. The Microsoft MSN Money Deluxe

Stock Screener software that we will use in this section is located at *http://moneycentral.msn.com/investor/finder/custom stocks.asp*. By inputting the criteria that we desire stock chart personalities to exhibit, we will be able to automatically harvest all stock that we seek. So what stock personality are you looking for?

Well, there are a few I like to use. They are as follows:

1. The Good Man (aka The Upward Trended)
2. The Bad Man (aka The Downward Trended)
3. The Over Comer (aka The Consolidator)
4. The Flyer (aka The High Volume Lift)
5. The Sleeper (aka The Price Breakout)
6. The Oscillator (aka the Channeller)
7. The Elastic Limit (aka 200-day MA Kisser)
8. The Marketers (aka The Indexes)
9. The Slug (aka The Large Caps)
10. The Overexcited and Over Priced (aka The Impending Stone)

Let us analyse them one by one.

The Good Man (aka the Upward Trended)

The Upward Trended chart belongs to stocks that have had one or more of the following criteria:

- Good earnings.
- Good news coverage.
- Great split point.
- Very strong fundamentals.
- Trading in the right sector/industry during a bull market.

Figure 56: The upward trended stock

You can spot these stocks a mile away; they have at least 12 months of upward trend. During that time, they never breach their 200-day MA. They have a strong and consistent trading volume, just like ERES in Figure 56.

To find the upward trended stocks with the MSN Money Deluxe Stock Screener, the criteria you want are as follows:

Field Name	Operator	Value
% Price Change YTD	>=	20
Next Yr Growth Rate	>=	25
Rev Growth YTD vs YTD	>=	20
Net Profit Margin	>=	10
Return on Equity	>=	15
12-Month Relative Stren...	>=	80
P/E Ratio: Current	>=	2

Figure 57: Criteria for upward trending stocks

Key in the details in Figure 57 and click Run Search.

The Bad Man (aka the Downward Trended)
This personality is the reverse of the Good Man. It belongs to companies that have had one or more of the following criteria:

- Bad earnings.
- Bad news coverage.
- Terrible split points.
- Very weak fundamentals.
- Trading in the wrong sector/industry during a bear market.

Figure 58: The downward trending stock

Calculating Fibonacci for the Downward Trending Stock

Again, you can spot these stocks from a long way off. They have crossed the 200-day MA, and tend to stay there most of the time. The strategy to use with this chart is to wait until the stock price is closest to the 200-day MA, then short the stock. You can get the most accurate point of entry by using Fibonacci. Looking at Figure 58, the calculations for the Fibonacci 61.8% line 1 and 2 are as follows:

$$\text{Fib } 1^6 = 37.74 + ((48.32 - 37.74) \times 0.618) = \$44.28$$
$$\text{Fib } 2 = 36.65 + ((42.45 - 36.65) \times 0.618) = \$40.24$$

To find the downward trended stocks with the MSN Money Deluxe Stock Screener, the criteria you want are illustrated below:

Key in the details in Figure 59, then click Run Search.

---

[6] Note that Fib 1 and Fib 2 represent the Fibonacci 61.8% lines marked in Figure 80.

Field Name	Operator	Value
% Price Change YTD	<=	20
Next Yr Growth Rate	<=	20
Rev Growth YTD vs YTD	<=	20
Net Profit Margin	<=	20
Return on Equity	<=	20
12-Month Relative Stren...	<=	20
ROI: 5-Year Avg.	<=	20
Avg. Daily Vol. Last Year	>=	1,000,000

Figure 59: Criteria for downward trending stocks

Figure 59 is a screener simply for stocks that are downward trending. However, in Figure 60, we see a screener for stocks that have just broken the 200-day MA. In addition, in Figure 60, we see a screener for stock that have just broken the 200-day MA, and carried on way past it.

Field Name	Operator	Value
% Price Change YTD	<=	20
Next Yr Growth Rate	<=	20
Rev Growth YTD vs YTD	<=	15
Net Profit Margin	<=	20
Return on Equity	<=	20
12-Month Relative Stren...	<=	20
ROI: 5-Year Avg.	<=	20
Avg. Daily Vol. Last Year	>=	100,000
50-Day Moving Average	<=	200-Day Moving Average
% Price Change YTD	<=	-30

Figure 60: Criteria for 200-day MA breakers

Field Name	Operator	Value
% Price Change YTD	Display Only	
Avg. Daily Vol. Last Year	>=	1,000,000
Previous Day's Closing Price	>=	0.2*200-Day Moving Average
Previous Day's Closing Price	<=	0.7*200-Day Moving Average
Last Price	>=	10
% Price Change Today	<=	-1

Figure 61: Criteria for 200-day MA deep diverse

The Over Comer (aka the Consolidator)

This is another sleeper personality. The only difference between the Over Comer and the Sleeper is that the Over Comer falls to new lows to consolidate, then attempts other highs or lows. You use the same trading advice as for the Sleeper.

Normally, the Over Comer has just come out of an all time high and fallen to the Fibonacci 61.8% level. Determine the channel and watch for a channel break. Trade this personality depending on the direction of the breakout (i.e. sell short if down, and buy long if up).

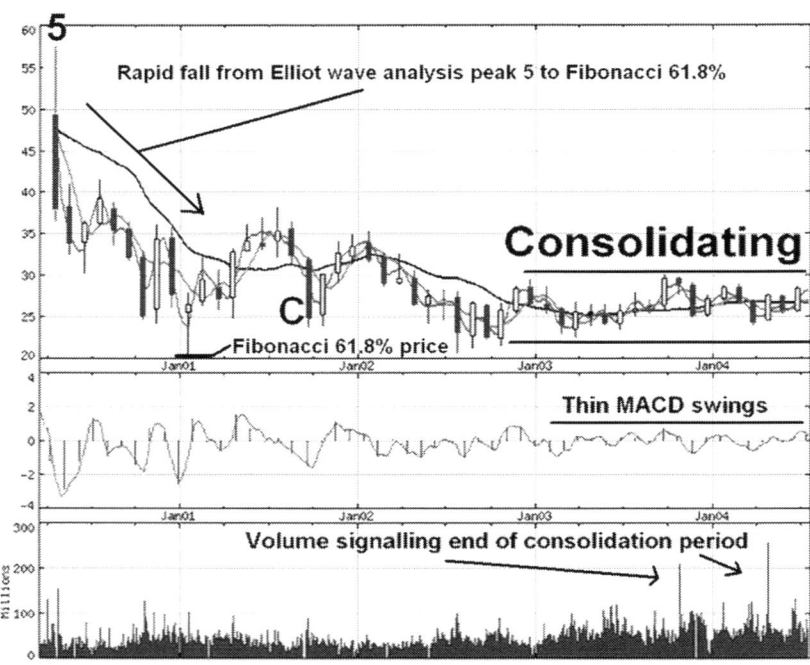

Figure 62: MSFT consolidating after Jan 2000

To find consolidator stocks with the MSN Money Deluxe Stock Screener, the criteria you want are as follows:

Field Name	Operator	Value
Last Price	<=	0.9*52-Week High
Market Capitalization	>=	100,000,000
Previous Day's Closing Price	>=	10
Avg. Daily Vol. Last Year	>=	1,000,000
% Price Change Last Qtr.	<=	2
% Price Change Last Qtr.	>=	0

Figure 63: Criteria for the Consolidator

The Flyer (aka the High Volume Lift)

The high volume lift technique is a very volatile technique. It should only be used by those who are able to follow instructions precisely, without wavering or amending any part of the original message. If you do not feel you are such a person, skip this technique.

Every now and then, a stock will pop up or down. Normally, when this happens, the pop lasts for a few days or perhaps a week before it reverses (see Elastic Limit chart, covered later in this appendix).

Figure 64: High volume single day surge

Single day highs

I have created a screener for you to take advantage of these pops. See Figure 65 for the correct criteria to use. As usual, key it into the MSN Money Deluxe Stock Screener, and then click Run Search.

81

The criteria specify that the volume change must be at least five times the daily average volume for the last two weeks. This incredible volume surge will keep the stock moving for a few days, perhaps longer. To reassure yourself that this is the going to last for a while, use Fibonacci to calculate the 61.8% line. To see the low accurately, you will have to view the 2-year chart (see Figure 68).

Field Name	Operator	Value
Last Volume	>=	5*Avg. Daily Vol. Last 2 Weeks
Last Price	>=	10
Market Capitalization	>=	1,000,000,000
Last Volume	>=	1,000,000

Figure 65: Criteria for the Flyer based on dramatic volume increase

52-day high

The second Flyer criteria shown in Figure 66, allow you to find stock with a high relative strength that is currently trading at 52-week highs. The way to trade these is simple; buy after the next pullback. See Figure 67.

Field Name	Operator	Value
Previous Day's Closing Price	>=	52-Week High
3-Month Relative Strength	>=	60
Avg. Daily Vol. Last Year	>=	10,000
Previous Day's Closing Price	>=	10

Figure 66: Criteria for the Flyer based on 52-week high

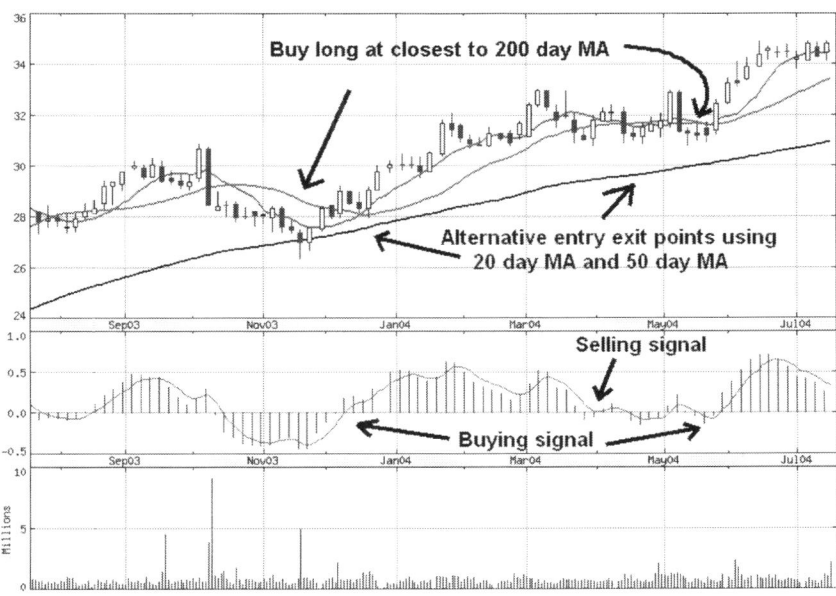

Figure 67: Flyer from 52-day high criteria

If the Flyer, just hit the 52-day high, you will need to watch it to see when the MACD and signal line touch the zero line, indicating a buy signal. This is a pullback.

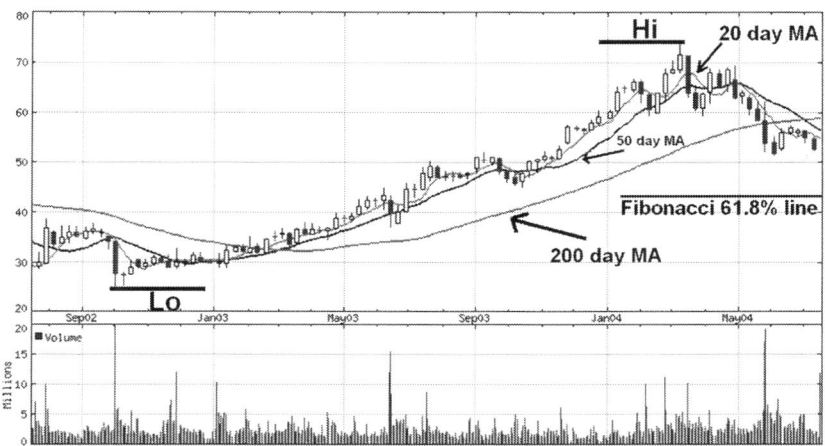

Figure 68: Calculating Fibonacci for GDT, a high volume Flyer

Calculating Fibonacci for the high volume Flyer

The calculation for the Fibonacci 61.8% line is as follows:

Fibonacci 61.8% line = 74.5 – ((74.5 – 25) x 0.618) = $43.91

As you can see from the chart above, the stock price is currently at $52. The stock will fall another $8.09. It is not worth getting into this stock yet, as you will loose 15% before it touches the Fibonacci line. Although you would recover your profit, it will just waste your time.

Here is how you trade the Flyer.

1. Use the screeners in Figure 65 or Figure 66 to harvest Flyer stocks.

2. Look at each of their charts on a one-year period to determine if you can make use of them. Remember that you are looking for stocks that have had the one-day volume rise on, or very near, their Fibonacci 61.8% rebound line.

3. Once you have selected the stocks that you think are ready, calculate the Fibonacci 61.8% line using either the upward trending or downward trending Fibonacci equations:

Hi – ((Hi - Lo) * 0.618) = If upwardly trending chart
Lo + ((Hi - Lo) * 0.618 = If downwardly trending chart

4. Set your price to buy or sell short at the Fibonacci line, or if you have just missed that, go for the current price with a limit order (see Placing Your Trades, on page 97, for how to buy stock).

5. Keep the stock until it passes the previous Hi used to calculate the Fibonacci line, and then sell 90% of it.

6. When the candlesticks indicate a reversal of the price, sell your remaining 10% of stock. In addition, take up a position using the opposite instrument, i.e. if you just came out of a long buy, then go for a short sell and visa versa. In this case, you want to sell the stock short, until it returns to another Fibonacci 61.8% line. You can do this securely because you can calculate where it will end.

In Figure 68, if you had not calculated the Fibonacci rebound line, you may have got into this stock either too late or too soon, and you would have lost time and money either way.

Note: if you are unsure about these instructions then do not trade this technique.

The Sleeper (aka the Price Breakout)

A Sleeper is a stock that oscillates in a relatively small channel in the hope of building up steam to fly higher or lower. These types of stocks are called Sleepers because they sleep (consolidate) for a long while, then move very fast in one direction. Sleepers are extremely profitable if you know how to spot them and accurately judge when they awake. Let us go straight into how to spot them and trade them.

Finding sleepers

The easiest way to find sleepers is to look for stocks that have been trading relatively thin price ranges within the last quarter. If you are viewing a one-year chart, this will be 3 months, if viewing a 6-month chart this will be 1 ½ months, if viewing a monthly chart this will be 1 week, if viewing a day chart this will be roughly 2 ½ days, and if viewing a 1 minute chart this will be 25 seconds.

I have created a one-year view Sleeper screener in Figure 70. As before, key these details into the MSN Money Deluxe Stock Screener, then click Run Search.

In the chart of Figure 69, you can se that this Sleeper was testing the low support established in November and December of 2003. The Sleeper tried to break out of the thin channel during January, February, and March of 2004. You would have known this would be unsuccessful because the pullbacks after these attempts were all roughly at the same price.

This means that the stock did not have the strength to establish new higher lows. After the third attempt in April 2004, it ran out of steam and returned to the support it had established earlier. It would seem that the attempt to break out had taken the steam out of this stock. It also tested the support four times, finally breaking through.

To trade this stock, you would have set a short sell order just below the support line. As the stock broke the support, your order would have filled, and you would have made a nice easy 10% gain in three or four days. As soon as you see the candlesticks turn white, you sell.

The link, *http://www.tradestars.com/grail-indicator.ASP* gives you a graphical indication of trend. It is useful if you want to check on a signal near the support or resistance lines. If the bars are red, it indicates a bearish trend, and if green, a bullish trend. However, you do not need this tool because you can draw your support lines and resistance lines from the first two successful tests of the same price. (Note that in Figure 69, no resistance line is established unlike in Figure 71). After drawing the lines (support and/or resistance), you simply wait for the price to cross.

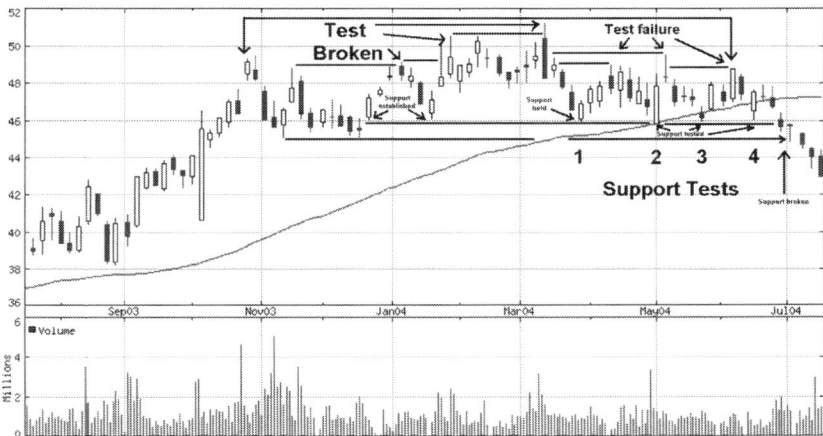

Figure 69: The sleeper awakes after testing the support four times

Field Name	Operator	Value
Last Price	>=	20
Last Volume	>=	10,000
Next Yr Growth Rate	>=	5
% Price Change Last Qtr.	<=	2
% Price Change Last Qtr.	>=	0
% Price Change Last Year	>=	25
Beta	<=	1
Market Capitalization	>=	1,000,000,000
% Price Change Last Month	<=	0.05

Figure 70: Sleeper screener criteria

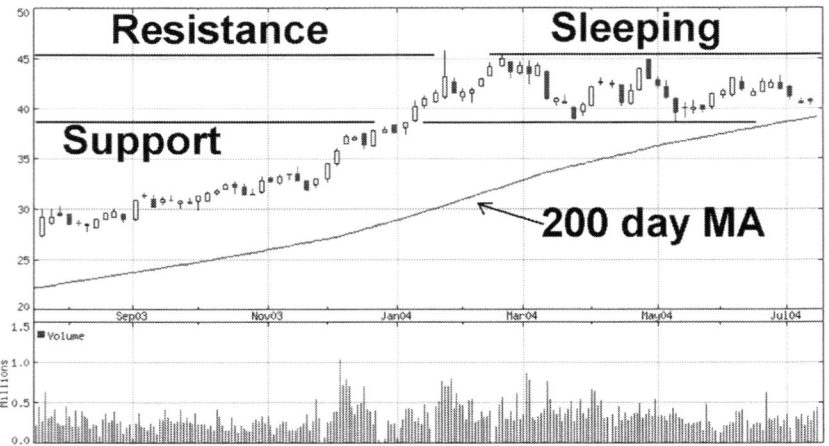

Figure 71: Sleeper breakout price limits

In Figure 71, you see a slumbering Sleeper. This stock is still sleeping but has established a support and resistance to form a small channel. When it breaks out, it will break either the resistance price or the support price. To trade this stock, all you need to do is to wait until it breaks $46 or $37. You can set up an alert via *http://www.stockalerts.com,* or use the alerting service supplied by Yahoo! Finance, or your broker. In Figure 71, if the price crossed $37, you would sell short. If the price were to cross $46 instead, you would have gone long and bought the stock.

Trading sleepers

Once you have found your Sleepers, analyse them to determine the channel resistance and support. Either watch the stock, or set up an alert to your email, phone, or pager, to alert you when it crosses either the support or the resistance line. If it crosses the resistance (top), then take a long position in the stock (buy it). If it crosses the support line (bottom), take a short position (sell short) in the stock.

The Oscillator (aka the Channeller)

Often, stock will oscillate in a small channel. This provides some interesting trading opportunities.

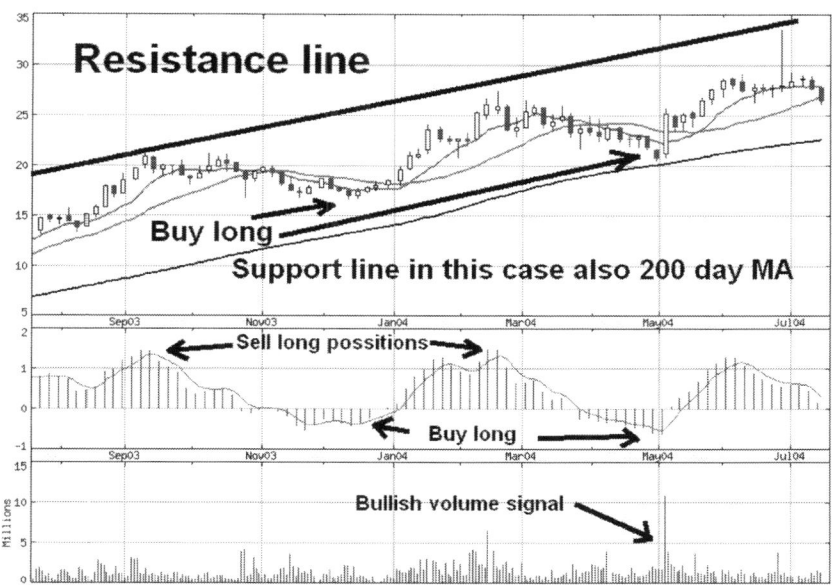

Figure 72: Oscillator or Channeller chart trending upwards

If the channel is upward trending, do the following:

1. Draw support and resistance lines.
2. Buy long at the support line and sell to close long positions at the resistance line.
3. Never go short in an upwardly trending channel.

Figure 73: Oscillator or Channeller chart trending downwards

If the channel is downward trending, do the following:

1. Draw support and resistance lines.
2. Sell short at the resistance line and buy to close short positions at the support line.
3. Never go long in a downwardly trending channel.

If the channel is moving sideways (no vertical trend), do the following:

4. Draw support and resistance lines.
5. Buy long at the support line and sell to close long positions at the resistance line.
6. Sell short at the resistance line and buy to close short positions at the support line.

The Elastic Limit (aka 200-day MA Kisser)

It is great to be able to trade a stock when you have a high degree of certainty that it will not go far past the 200-day MA. This is what the Elastic Limit, also known as the Kisser, does. It comes close enough to the 200-day MA to touch, but will rush back as if attached to an elastic band. To play this chart technique, use the screener provided to harvest stocks that qualify for this technique.

In Figure 74, you see a chart of a stock that moves from the 200-day MA line and then springs back again. Often, the distance a stock can stretch away from the 200-day MA is 3 times its normal sitting position above the 200-day MA. With this in mind, you would sell the stock once it is roughly three times its normal distance from the 200-day MA.

When buying this stock, you would purchase it at the closest point it gets to the 200-day MA on either side, or on the 200-day MA. The last point varies from stock to stock. To better judge entry point, keep an eye on the candlesticks for your clue. When the stock goes back to the 200-day MA or near it, and the candlesticks turn white, it is time to consider getting back in.

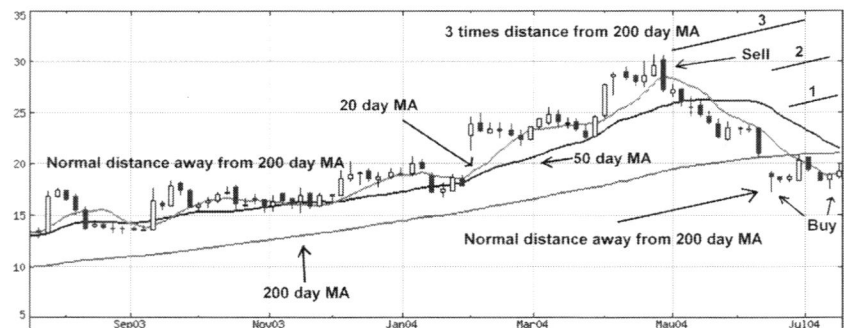

Figure 74: The Elastic Limit applied

The criteria for harvesting Elastic Limit stock above the 200-day moving MA, and on the 200-day MA, are illustrated in Figure 75 and Figure 76, respectively:

Field Name	Operator	Value
% Price Change YTD	Display Only	
Avg. Daily Vol. Last Year	>=	500,000
Previous Day's Closing Price	<=	5*200-Day Moving Average
Last Price	>=	1.5*200-Day Moving Average
Last Price	>=	10
% Price Change Today	<=	0

Figure 75: Criteria for Elastic limit away from 200-day MA

Field Name	Operator	Value
% Price Change YTD	Display Only	
Next Yr Growth Rate	>=	15
Rev Growth YTD vs YTD	>=	15
Net Profit Margin	>=	10
Return on Equity	>=	10
12-Month Relative Strength	>=	70
P/E Ratio: Current	>=	1

Figure 76: Criteria for Elastic limit over or on 200-day MA

This technique can be used in reverse; however, I have not given you screener criteria for this. You can use the Bad Man screener to select bearish stock charts for this technique. See Figure 77.

Figure 77: The Elastic Limit applied below 200-day MA

Calculating Fibonacci for the Elastic Limit

Fibonacci has been applied here to get the short sell entry points.

The Fibonacci calculations are as follows:

Fibonacci 61.8% line (using Hi and Lo)
$36.9 + ((48.9-36.9) \times 0.618) = \$44.32$

Fibonacci 61.8% line (using Hi 1 and Lo 1)
$36.7 + ((43.2-36.7) \times 0.618) = \$40.72$

You can also see that the exit points (where you buy to close the position), are signalled by the candlesticks turning white (see Lo and Lo 1).

The Marketers (aka the Indexes)

You can trade the Exchange Traded Funds (ETFs) for the major markets (i.e. QQQQ for the NASDAQ, SPY for the S&P, IWM for the Russell 2000, and DIA for the Dow Jones Industrial Average).

The great thing about trading an ETF is the huge volumes. They give you a thinner market maker spread and allow you to see clearer signals in charts. Each ETF is an instrument that represents a large amount of stocks as one stock. You can do with ETFs all you can do with stocks. This includes buying long, selling short, and trading their derivatives.

So why would you want to trade ETFs? Simply, for clear signalling. I like to go long and short on the DIA and SPY. This is because they give you the clearest 10 and 20 day MA signalling.

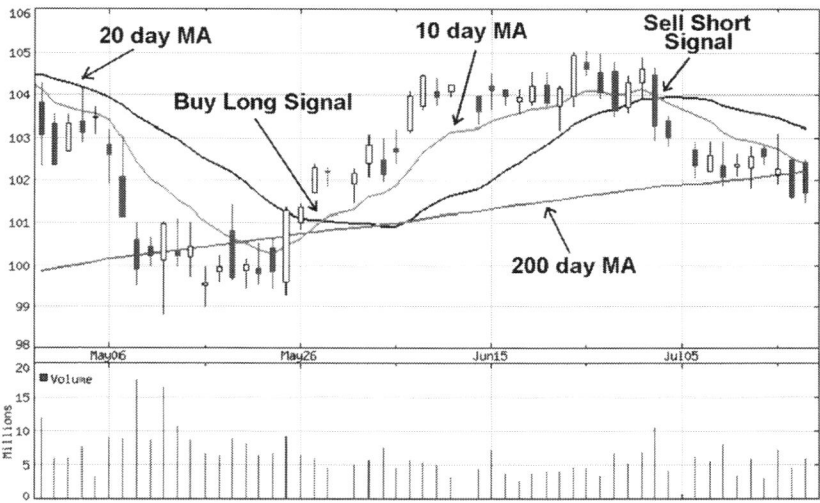

Figure 78: MA signalling with the DIA

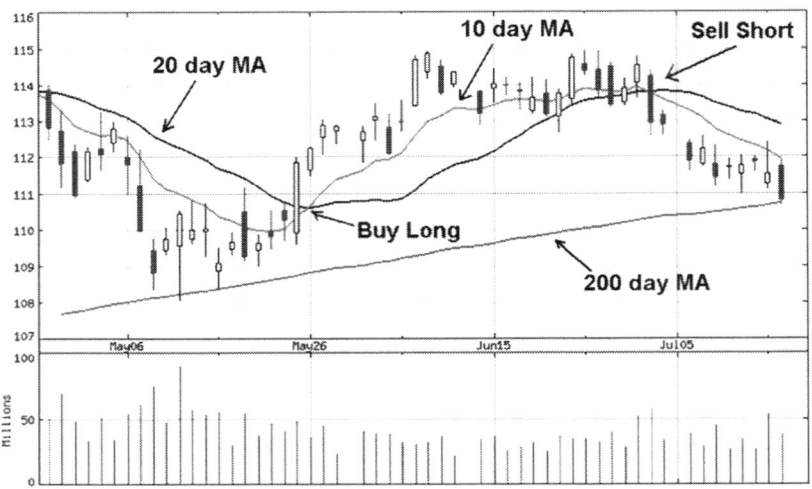

Figure 79: MA signalling with the SPY

Note how clear the signalling is in the SPY and DIA charts? When the 10 and 20-day MAs cross, they separate, giving a clear signal to buy or sell.

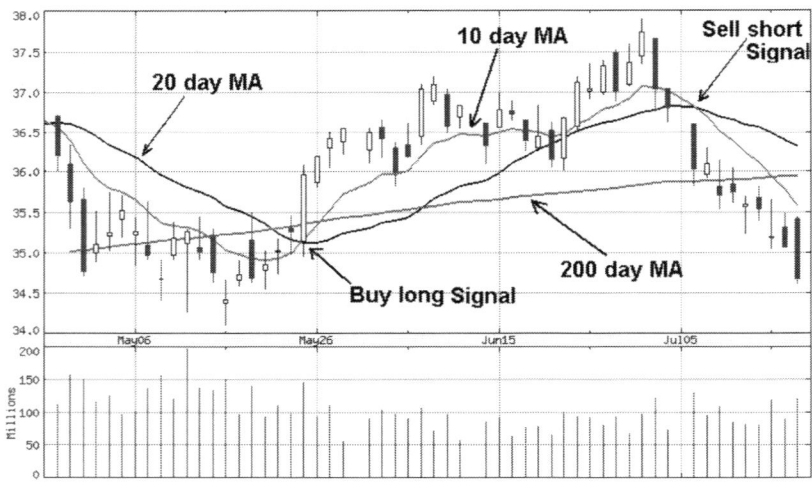

Figure 80: MA signalling with the QQQQ

The other ETFs are not always so clear in their MA signalling. See the QQQQ chart in Figure 80. The 10-day MA almost crossed the 20-day MA in the tail end of June 2004.

The 10% a month technique

Here a few points for trading ETFs below:

- Only trade DIA and SPY with this technique.
- Use a 3-month chart with 10 and 20-day MA indicators.
- When the MAs cross with the 10-day MA on top (10 day is higher than 20-day MA), close any short positions (buy to close your sell shorts) that you have in the ETF, then take a long position (buy long).
- When the opposite occurs, first sell your long positions in the ETF, and then take a short position (sell short).
- Aim for a 5% gain either way (long and short).

You can use an alerting service to warn you when the 10 and 20-day MAs cross. Try *http://alerts.yahoo.com*, *http://www.stockalerts.com,* or the alerting service provided by your broker.

The Slug (aka the Large Caps)

The Slug, also known as a Large Cap, is a very big corporation with billions of market capitalisation (available shares multiplied by the share price). Because these stocks are so big, they tend to react slower than the smaller companies do. Large Caps behave like the ETFs we discussed earlier.

Using Fibonacci, Elliot Wave theory, and the 20-day and 50-day MAs against the stocks from the criteria in Figure 82, you can get in on Large Cap stocks through their Elliot Wave C through to 5. This play can often earn you 25% to 100% gains in 12 months just in Large Caps alone. Let us see how this is done.

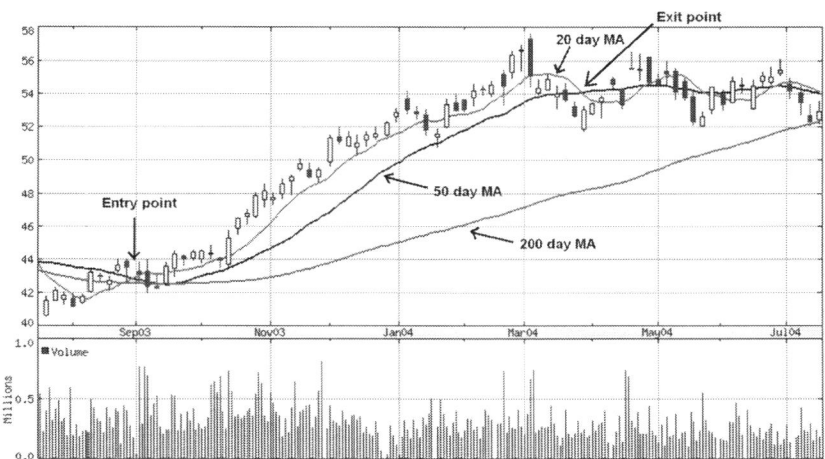

Figure 81: Large Cap entry and exit points

1. First, use the screener to harvest a selection of appropriate Large Cap stocks.

2. Look through 12-month charts of the Large Cap stock for Entry points. An entry point is a point in a stock chart where the 50 and 20-day MAs cross either on or very near the 200-day MA.

3. Wait until the cross is over and the stock price is higher than the 20-day MA. Make sure the 20 day MA is high than the 50 day MA. Finally, make sure that the 50-day MA is higher than the 200-day MA (see Figure 81).

4. Go long in the stock (buy it), and wait for the 20-day and 50-day MAs to cross.
5. When the 50-day and 20-day MAs cross, sell your long position, and look for another Large Cap that is ready for this technique.

There are a few things to watch out for with this technique. Be patient, as it may take a month or two for the stock to be ready for your entry. Do not rush; find another Large Cap that is ready to apply this technique with if you cannot wait until then.

Field Name	Operator	Value
Current Dividend Yield	>=	2
Market Capitalization	>=	25,000,000,000
Current Ratio	>=	Industry Average Current Ratio
Debt to Equity Ratio	<=	Industry Average Debt to Equity Ratio
Previous Day's Closing Price	>=	0.9*52-Week High
Last Price	Near	200-Day Moving Average

Figure 82: Criteria for Picking Slugs

This technique is only to be used with stock from the criteria in Figure 82. DO NOT USE THIS TECHINQUE TO SELL STOCK SHORT.

The Overexcited and Over Priced (aka the Impending Stone)

Field Name	Operator	Value
Previous Day's Closing Price	>=	52-Week High
3-Month Relative Strength	>=	80
Avg. Daily Vol. Last Year	>=	100,000
P/E Ratio: Current	>=	10
Previous Day's Closing Price	>=	10

Figure 83: Criteria for picking the Overexcited and Over Priced stocks

To trade Overexcited and Over Priced stocks, use the criteria from Figure 83 to harvest the stocks. Select the chart that has the current price closest to the 200-day MA (i.e. a chart of a stock in the process of doing a pull back. See Figure 84 for buy long entry points). Go long in that stock and wait until you see a peak in the MACD chart. When the MACD stops sitting above the signal line, sell your stocks and wait. Do not go short in these stocks. Never short Overexcited and Over Priced stocks unless they break out below the 200-day MA Then and only then should you calculate the Fibonacci 61.8% price, and short the stock until that price is reached (within 2% tolerance).

As long as the pullbacks to the 200-day MA reverse without crossing the 200-day MA, go long again (see Figure 84).

Figure 84: **Criteria**
for picking **The**

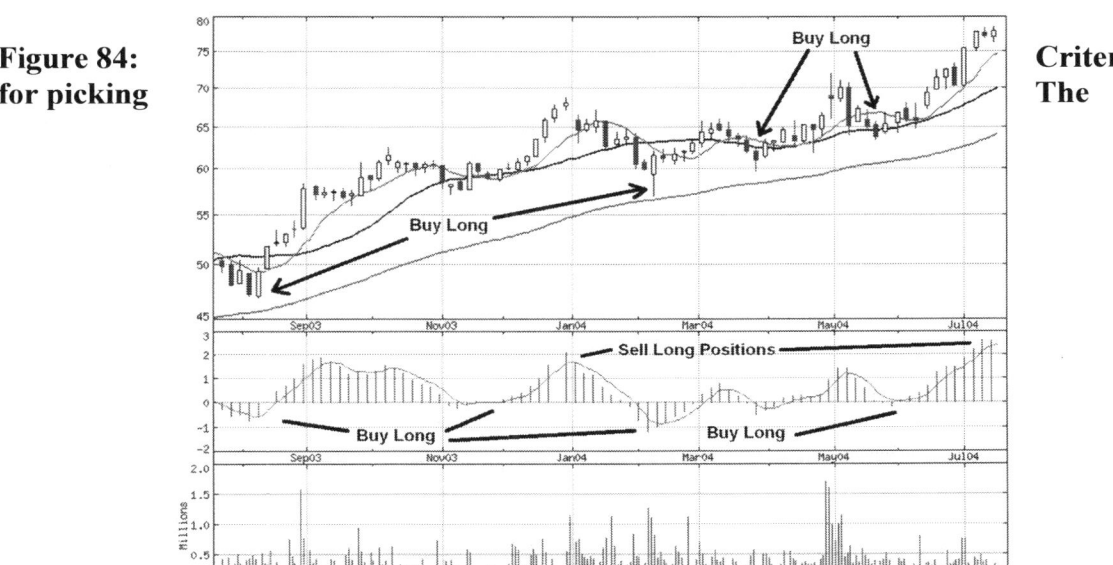

Overexcited and Over Priced stocks

Placing Your Trades

You can place your trade with a broker via phone, fax, email, or on the internet. Most Brokerage firms only take orders via the internet or phone. The cheapest method is normally via the internet. You will need to know the symbol for the stock you want to buy. There are several options you have when placing your trade. These are as follows:

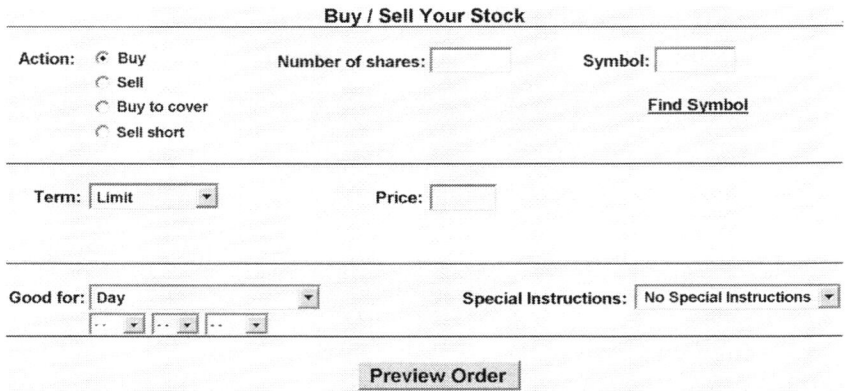

Figure 85: Example of an order form

Action – this is where you specify whether you want to buy (long) shares or sell (short) shares. If you already own the stock, you can specify to Sell. If you have sold short and want to Buy to Cover, you can also do this.

Number of Shares – In this section of the order form, you specify how many shares of the stock you want to buy. If you were spending your total balance, this would be:

(Your account balance – commission charges) /price of stock = Number of shares you can afford.

If you are using margin as well as your account balance, add the margin value to your account balance, and use this as your account balance in the equation above.

Symbol – type the stocks symbol here (i.e. MSFT or GE etc). If you do not know the symbol but know the company name, your broker's order page will have a find symbol button to allow you to find the companies symbol.

Term – This may also be called order type. This is where you select from one of the following:

- *Market*. Select this type of order if you want to purchase at the current market price. You have to select good for day, in the Good for section
- *Limit* Select this type of order if you want to buy at a specified price when the share price reaches a fixed price. You have to specify this price. This specified price has to be greater than the current price if a long order, and less than the current price if a short order.
- *Stop Market* Select this type of order if you want to place a market order when the price gets to a set price.
- *Stop Limit* Select this type of order if you want to place a limit order when the price gets to a set price.

- ***Trailing Stop*** Select this type of order if you want to place a stop limit at a set point, or a percentage behind the current price. Keep moving this stop limit as the stock moves in price. Not all brokers may offer this option.

Price – if you selected any term except Market, you will need to specify a price.

Good for – this is where you specify how long you want the order to stay active. You can select one of the following:

- ***Day*** – Your order will stay open until end of the trading day. Normally, market orders are filled within seconds of placing them. (This option must be selected when placing a market order).
- ***Market on close (MOC)*** – This is a buy or sell order which is to be executed as a market order as close as possible to the end of the day.
- ***End of week (EOW)*** – This order lasts until end of trading on Friday.
- ***End of month (EOM)*** – This order stays open until end of day, on the last trading day of the month.
- ***Good until cancelled (GTC)*** – This order stays open for 90 days.
- ***Good through date (GTD)*** – This order stays open through the date you specify.

Special instructions – This is where you specify any other instructions you want associated with the order. You will normally be presented with the following list:

- No special instruction.
- All or none (AON) – Fill all your order or none of it.
- Do not reduce (DNR) – Do not fill in smaller batches.
- Fill or kill (FOK) – Fill the order or cancel the order.
- AON/DNR – Fill all or none/do not fill in smaller bathes.

Once you have specified all the order criteria, you can preview your order and confirm it if the preview is correct. Market orders are the cheapest order type. I never use market orders because I find the market makers always sell market orders at a premium. The only time this is not true is when buying large caps or blue chips. These companies have such huge volumes that the market makers can afford to have smaller margins.

Main points to remember

Never use market orders, always use a limit order, and specify the price you wish to purchase. Never be in a hurry to own a stock. You make mistakes when you are desperate. During the day, the stock price will fluctuate to its daily highs and its daily lows. Always aim to buy at discount. Set the price to what you calculated through your Fibonacci or other indicator, and place a limit order to catch the stock at that price. In a very short period, you will discover that you actually made a handsome profit by not using market orders. As your profits and investments grow, the commission for your trades will shrink in comparison with your investments size.

Final Words On Stocks And Shares

From this Appendix 2, you can see that with the mastery of very few skills, you can become extremely profitable in your trading. The skills that you will need to master are listed below:

1. Applying asset allocation (see Appendix 3 for more information)
2. Using stock screeners
3. Drawing channels
4. Reading candlesticks
5. Using moving averages
6. Using volume signals
7. Using MACD and signal lines
8. Applying Elliot Wave Analysis to stock charts
9. Calculating Fibonacci lines
10. Buying long and selling short

Before you go live and start using real money, apply to one of the virtual portfolios offered by your broker, or MSN Money, or Yahoo! Finance. You can build a portfolio there by trading real stocks with virtual money. If you find you are making double digit profits in ten successive trades, then you may be ready to use your hard-earned cash to trade.

For information on trading games and virtual portfolios, see the following websites:

1. Bloomberg.com
   http://www.bloomberg.com/mag/pjump.html?sidenav=front

2. Briefing.com
   http://fast.quote.com/fq/briefing/fqportfolio?mode=quote&page=port

3. Zacks.com
   http://my.zacks.com/index.php3

4. MSN Money
   http://moneycentral.msn.com/investor/controls/setup.asp?Symbol=&target=/investor/charts/charting.asp

5. Forbes.com: Tools
   http://www.forbes.com/tools

6. Barchart.com

http://equities.barchart.com/portfolio.htx

7. ClearStation.com
   http://www.clearstation.com/cgi-bin/drill_portfolio

8. Financial Times
9. *http://mwportfolio.ft.com/custom/ft-com/portfolio/view.asp*

10. QuoteTracker.com
    http://www.QuoteTracker.com

11. NASDAQ.com
    http://www.nasdaq.com/asp/portfoliojava.asp?

12. TheStreet.com
    http://www.thestreet.com/tsc/moneynetland.html

13. Yahoo! Finance
    http://finance.yahoo.com/?u

14. Raging Bull
    http://finance.lycos.com/home/portfolio/intro.asp

15. CBS MarketWatch
    http://cbs.marketwatch.com/portfolio/default.asp?siteid=mktw

16. Silicon Investor
    http://www.siliconinvestor.com/customize/login.gsp?ret=%2Fportfolio%2Findex.gsp

17. StockHouse.com
    http://www.stockhouse.com/members/login.asp?url=../portfolio/index.asp

18. MSN Money
    http://moneycentral.msn.com/scripts/webquote.dll?iPage=pmx

19. Briefing.com
    http://fast.quote.com/fq/briefing/fqportfolio_edit

20. Stockpoint.com
    http://www.stockpoint.com/leftnav/login.asp

21. Auditrack.com
    http://auditrack.com/

I hope you will take a small part of your buy and hold allocation (20% maximum), and trade one of the screeners we looked at in this appendix. By carefully following the instructions and rules of entry and exit for each of the personalities given, and making sure you use STOP LIMIT orders to protect your positions, you will have great success and make double digit profits from stock trading.

Appendix 3

Asset Allocation

Applying asset allocation principles to your investment portfolio will not only decrease the effects of disasters, but will help you take advantage of the inherent opportunities hidden within disasters. For instance, during a market crash, if you applied asset allocation to your investments, you would have the vast majority of your investments in secure assets that would be untouched by the market crash. Therefore, when others are wiped out, and equity and property prices are at an all time low, you can use some of your secure investments to snap up these bargains, thus reaping great profits when the market later recovers.

This is the purpose and benefit of a good asset allocated portfolio. If you do not begin with this, you could end up as I did in 2000, starting from scratch because an unexpected disaster like the March 2000 stock market crash befell me. Take heed to this wise advice. Start by allocating assets to the four categories: security, buy and hold, momentum, and lifestyle.

The only category I will not cover is Lifestyle, as it requires no help from me for you to spend your money. Notice that I left this category until last. This should be the last category to put your money in, as financially, it is a hole in the ground. Cars, designer clothes, holidays, electronic gadgets etc, will not return any interest. In some cases as with cars and private jets, they will actually cost you money to keep them. In addition to this, aim to use returns from investments to increase your lifestyle, not your salary or main income.

The proper allocation of investment funds to assets can be achieved by taking your age and current financial position into consideration. So let us get started and learn what each investment category is, and how much to allocate to it.

The three investment categories that we will now cover will be as follows:

- Security
- Buy and hold
- Momentum

Security

Security products protect you against a negative downside.[7] Examples of these are a will, life insurance, critical illness insurance, health plan, pension plan, and tax-exempt savings instruments.

Buy And Hold

These are assets both with or without tax-exemption, and with potential for a negative downside. These products do not qualify for the security category. Examples of them are shares, fine wine, diamonds, funds, and bonds, etc. These products generally have a maximum loss potential of your investment in them, as you can only loose what you put in them at the worst case.

Momentum

Momentum consists of assets with a high risk factor, offering potentially high positive upside returns, as well as potentially high negative downside losses i.e. options, futures, and spread betting etc. These products may have an unlimited loss potential as you could loose more than you originally invested in them.

Applying Asset Allocation

You should aim to invest most of your assets and investment income into security products and investments that are free from a negative downside. In addition to that, all investments in the security category should also be exempt from tax. We will now look at the two key considerations for determining how you apply asset allocation. These two factors are age and current financial state.

Age
Below 30

If you are at below 30 (the furthest group away from retirement age), you may want to increase your buy and hold and momentum allocations to lean more on the riskier side, as you have the time to recover from potential disasters to your buy and hold and momentum assets.

---

[7] Financial instruments grow in value or decrease in value. When they have the potential to grow in value, we say that they have a positive upside. When they have the potential to decrease in value, we say that have a negative downside.

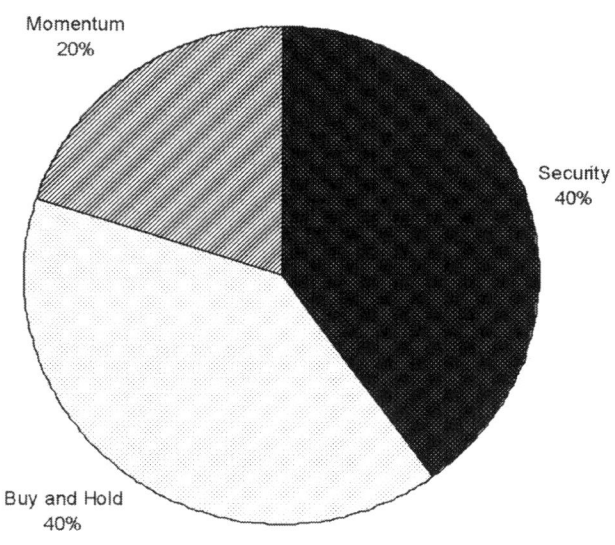

Figure 1-1: Furthest from retirement age - asset allocation (below 30)

30 to 50

Those in the middle-aged group of 30 to 50 should consider a more middle ground asset allocation style. Neither too risky nor too security focused.

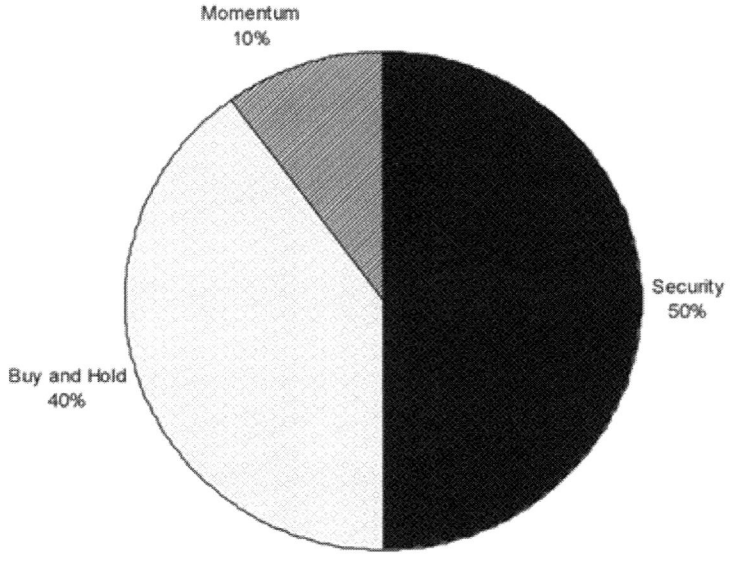

Figure 1-2: Middle-aged - asset allocation (30 to 50)

50 plus

Those of you who are 50 plus, and therefore close to retirement age, should increase your security allocations and decrease your riskier assets.

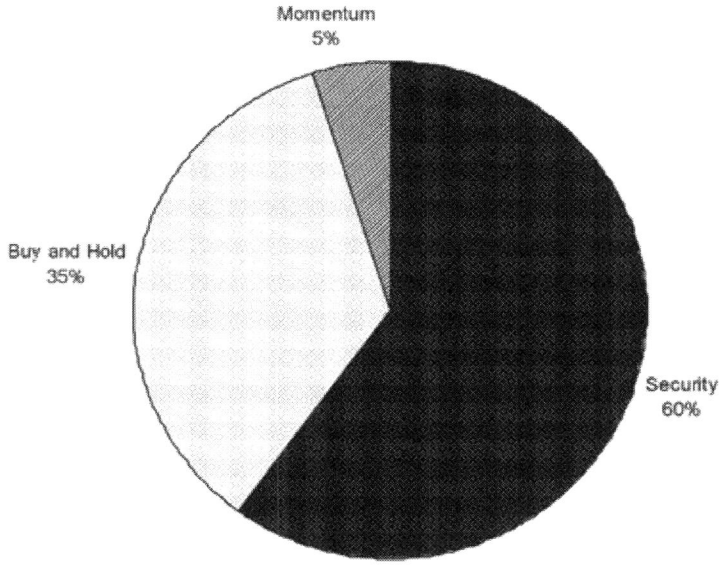

Figure 1-3: Near retirement age - asset allocation (50 plus)

I mentioned earlier that there were two considerations. You have looked at the first one, age. Now let us look at the second, your current financial state.

Current Financial State
We will break this section into three groups: the poor, the wealth off, and the rich.
The poor
These people should not invest in anything but security products and investments, as they cannot afford any downside risk. It does not matter how much money you earn, if you spend more than you are making then you should only invest into security products and investments (if you have any disposable income available).

Note: If you are in this category, you can get out of it by reading and applying the advice in the prequel to this book, *How to Destroy Your Debts*. Until you are no longer in this category, you should not invest in any buy and hold or momentum products, or investments.

The well off

The second group, the well off, are those who spend less than they make and have no debt, except perhaps a mortgage. If you are in this group, you will have disposable income and thus can afford to invest into buy and hold investments. For this group of people I would advise you applying the asset allocation of Figure 1-1. Until you are free from all debt, which includes your mortgage, you should not invest into any momentum products or investments.

Note: Incidentally, reading and applying *How to Destroy Your Debts* would also help those in this category, especially in clearing your mortgage in a fraction of the normal time it would otherwise take.

The rich

Those who have no debt and spend less than they make, will be able to use the age considerations covered previously, to decide how to allocate their assets.

Therefore, you can afford a little risk if you have no debts and are living within your means. A maximum of 20% of your assets (although 5%-10% is recommended), and investment income can be allocated to momentum[8]. Make sure however, that you do not lower your security allocation below 40%, no matter what your situation.

Other Considerations

If you are contemplating placing yourself in the wrong category, i.e. the Rich category, when you currently belong in another category, i.e. the poor category, you will only be delaying the time it takes to become totally financially free. You could also be worsening your situation and inviting disaster to befall you.

Do not invest more into momentum, thinking you will catch up with your security assets when you have made a fortune. You will only worsen matters, or worse still, you could end up bankrupt. If you do not want to apply the advice in this section on Asset Allocation, please do not read any further, as you can only do yourself harm.

Learn from the Egyptian pyramids. They have lasted over thousands of years because they were made to last the test of time. Make sure that your foundation for total financial freedom is made up of security products and investments. Figure 1-4 below illustrates the ideal secure and sturdy structure formed when this balance is implemented through correct asset allocation. As you can see, the pyramid is secure resting on a base of security. Once this secure base is established, you can build the next level on top, buy and hold. Finally, you complete your asset allocation with a small allocation into momentum products.

---

[8] Figure 1-1, Figure 1-2 and Figure 1-3 are based on the maximum allocations.

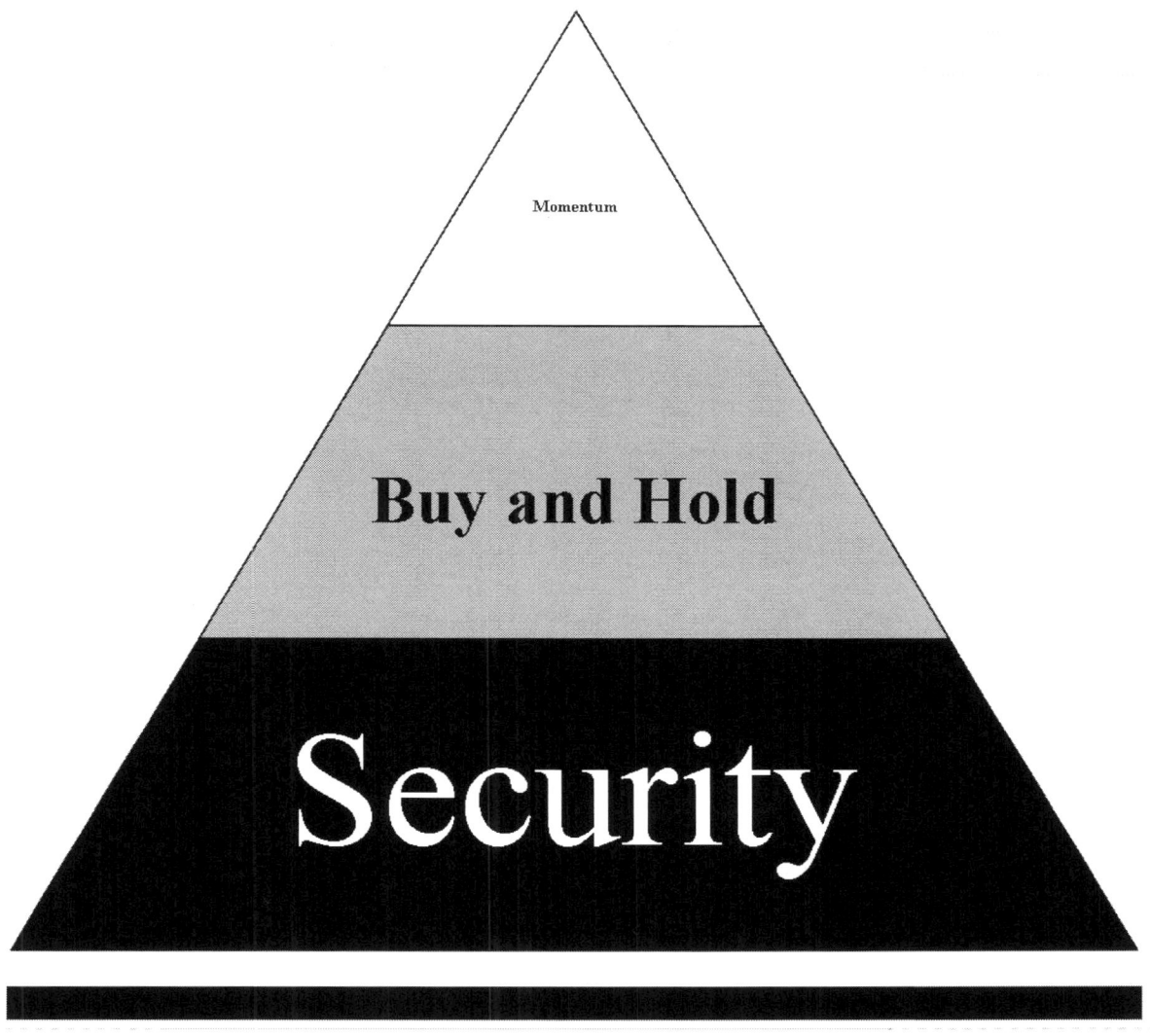

Figure 1-4: Ideal balanced asset allocation (N.B. momentum is represented by the white triangle above buy and hold)

In Figure 1-5, you can see that you will have a weak base if you invest more in buy and hold, and less in security. This structure will not stand for long. It would only take a stock market crash, or economic downturn, and your whole investment structure would topple.

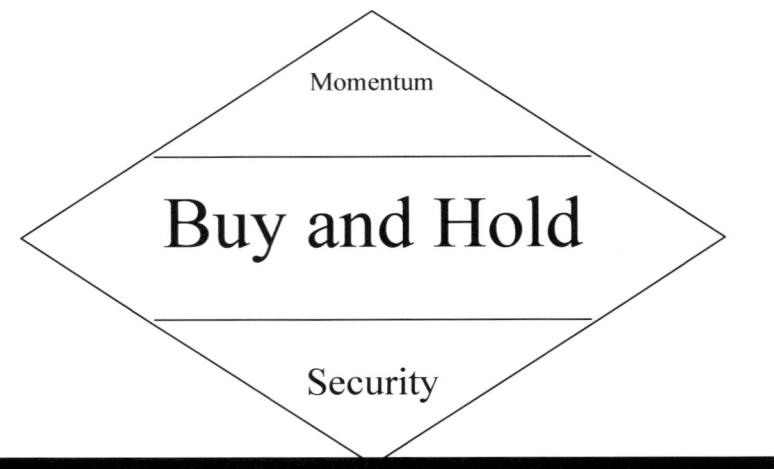

Figure 1-5: Over-investment in buy and hold

Looking at Figure 1-6 below, you will see the most volatile and dangerous structure you could build. By having most of your investments in momentum products, with few of your assets in security, you stand a chance of being completely wiped out by the slightest unexpected turn in the markets.

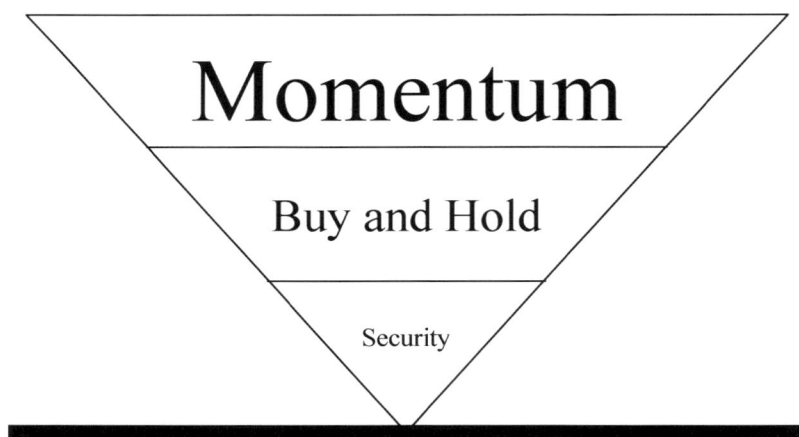

Figure 1-6: Over-investment into momentum

Notes

Other Works By Samuel Blankson

How to Destroy Your Debts

Printed: 165 pages, 6.0 x 9.0 in, Perfect-bound
Download: PDF (1739 kb)
ISBN: 1-4116-2374-6
Copyright Year: © 2005 by Samuel Blankson
Language: English
Publisher: Lulu.com

If you are like me, you hate being in debt! Every month you watch, your money run out before the end of the month. You scrape around for fuel and grocery money, and then finally you hit the credit cards, hoping they hold sufficient funds. If you want to get out of this cycle of worry over debt, this book may be your answer. I say, "May," because although this book will definitely give you techniques for controlling, managing, and even getting out of debt altogether, it will not do the work for you. That will be up to you. This book will reveal how to destroy your debts, including your mortgage. It will also make clear to you how you can increase your income, and have confidence in your financial future. Your journey to financial freedom begins here.

The Practical Guide to Total Financial Freedom: Volume 1

Printed: 124 pages, 8.5 x 11.0 in, Perfect-bound
Download: PDF (7761 kb)
ISBN: 1-4116-2058-5
Copyright Year: © 2005 by Samuel Blankson
Language: English
Publisher: Lulu.com

The first part of a five volume series on creating Total Financial Freedom. In this volume, you will learn the foundations of wealth building, and how to secure your family and your wealth against disasters and losses. This series offers practical, effective, and easy to follow advice for securely and quickly building wealth. If you are thinking of buying this book, you probably want to be free. Free from the rat race, free from the boss, free from the wage trap, and free from the mediocrity and hopelessness of poverty and lack of options. Until now, you may have had no other way of achieving this within the next half a decade. This book will change all that forever. This book, unlike many self-help books out there, will actually tell you what to do in order to achieve Total Financial Freedom. You will find out exactly how I went about achieving Total Financial Freedom. If you read, learn, and apply the lessons in this book, you too will achieve Total Financial Freedom.

The Practical Guide to Total Financial Freedom: Volume 2

Printed: 173 pages, 8.5 x 11.0 in, Perfect-bound
Download: PDF (31040 kb)
ISBN: 1-4116-2057-7
Copyright Year: © 2005 by Samuel Blankson
Language: English
Publisher: Lulu.com

The second part of a five volume series on creating Total Financial Freedom. In this volume, you will learn how to invest in Bonds, Stocks and Shares, and Funds. This series offers practical, effective, and easy to follow advice for securely and quickly building wealth. If you are thinking of buying this book, you probably want to be free. Free from the rat race, free from the boss, free from the wage trap, and free from the mediocrity and hopelessness of poverty and lack of options. Until now, you may have had no other way of achieving this within the next half a decade. This book will change all that forever. This book, unlike many self-help books out there, will actually tell you what to do in order to achieve Total Financial Freedom. You will find out exactly how I went about achieving Total Financial Freedom. If you read, learn, and apply the lessons in this book, you too will achieve Total Financial Freedom.

The Practical Guide to Total Financial Freedom: Volume 3

Printed: 143 pages, 8.5 x 11.0 in, Perfect-bound
Download: PDF (1716 kb)
ISBN: 1-4116-2056-9
Copyright Year: © 2005 by Samuel Blankson
Language: English
Publisher: Lulu.com

The third part of a five volume series on creating Total Financial Freedom. In this volume, you will learn how to invest in En Primeur Wine, Real Estate, Businesses, Life Insurances, Art, and Offshore investment opportunities. This series offers practical, effective, and easy to follow advice for securely and quickly building wealth. If you are thinking of buying this book, you probably want to be free. Free from the rat race, free from the boss, free from the wage trap, and free from the mediocrity and hopelessness of poverty and lack of options. Until now, you may have had no other way of achieving this within the next half a decade. This book will change all that forever. This book, unlike many self-help books out there, will actually tell you what to do in order to achieve Total Financial Freedom. You will find out exactly how I went about achieving Total Financial Freedom. If you read, learn, and apply the lessons in this book, you too will achieve Total Financial Freedom.

The Practical Guide to Total Financial Freedom: Volume 4

Printed: 134 pages, 8.5 x 11.0 in, Perfect-bound
Download: PDF (3961 kb)
ISBN: 1-4116-2055-0
Copyright Year: © 2005 by Samuel Blankson
Language: English
Publisher: Lulu.com

The fourth part of a five volume series on creating Total Financial Freedom. In this volume, you will learn how to trade and invest in Momentum products. These instruments are high-risk products that offer high returns, but also the possibilities of high losses. You will learn how to limit those losses by reducing the risk using effective and practical methods. Options, Futures, High Yield Investment Programs, and Gambling are some of the exciting topics covered in detail. This series offers practical, effective, and easy to follow advice for securely and quickly building wealth. This book, unlike many self-help books out there, will actually tell you what to do in order to achieve Total Financial Freedom. You will find out exactly how I went about achieving Total Financial Freedom. If you read, learn, and apply the lessons in this book, you too will achieve Total Financial Freedom.

The Practical Guide to Total Financial Freedom: Volume 5

Printed: 322 pages, 8.5 x 11.0 in, Perfect-bound
Download: PDF (7143 kb)
ISBN: 1-4116-2054-2
Copyright Year: © 2005 by Samuel Blankson
Language: English
Publisher: Lulu.com

The last part of a five volume series on creating Total Financial Freedom. In this volume, you will learn how to lower your taxes, avoid paying unfair and unnecessary taxes, and how to move offshore and pay no taxes at all. This series offers practical, effective, and easy to follow advice for securely and quickly building wealth. If you are thinking of buying this book, you probably want to be free. Free from the rat race, free from the boss, free from the wage trap, and free from the mediocrity and hopelessness of poverty and lack of options. Until now, you may have had no other way of achieving this within the next half a decade. This book will change all that forever. This book, unlike many self-help books out there, will actually tell you what to do in order to achieve Total Financial Freedom. You will find out exactly how I went about achieving Total Financial Freedom. If you read, learn, and apply the lessons in this book, you too will achieve Total Financial Freedom.

Living the Ultimate Truth, 2nd Edition

Printed: 166 pages, 6.0 x 9.0 in, Perfect-bound
Download: PDF (855 kb)
ISBN: 1-4116-2375-4
Copyright Year: © 2005 by Samuel Blankson
Language: English
Publisher: Lulu.com

Today most people live a poor example of a balanced life. The centuries of wisdom passed down from the great leaders of our past seem lost amid lives centred on minutia and selfishness. Today we care more about what we wear and where we are seen, than we do about discovering and Living the Ultimate Truth. Throughout the world, there is an imbalance in people's spirituality, consciousness, and inner harmony. This has taken a great toll on our environment, our health, and our happiness. Many are wondering around like lost sheep, seeking a shepherd in all the wrong places. Many false prophets have promised quick fixes to these problems, but if these solutions are not firmly rooted in The Creator, love, integrity and inner harmony, they are doomed to fail. This book is a reminder of all those virtues and universal principles that we need, to return to a balanced, harmonious, and happy life. You will learn to love yourself, love others, and finally find that inner peace you seek through spiritual growth.

Developing Personal Integrity, 2nd Edition

Printed: 118 pages, 6.0 x 9.0 in, Perfect-bound
Download: PDF (627 kb)
ISBN: 1-4116-2376-2
Copyright Year: © 2005 by Samuel Blankson
Language: English
Publisher: Lulu.com

In the field of human character development, integrity is the last frontier. Many people use the word, but few really know what real integrity is. This book breaks down the fundamental components of personal integrity and offers a path to attaining it. Like success or happiness, integrity is a journey not a destination. We can only measure how far on the path we are through the observation of our inner voice, the voice of our conscience, and through deep contemplation and reflection. This journey of personal excellence is not an easy one, and as a friend once said, "When peeling this onion, sometimes you cry." Nevertheless, in all great endeavours, the harder the struggle, the greater the victory will be.

The Guide to Real Estate Investing

Printed: 117 pages, 6.0 x 9.0 in, Perfect-bound
Download: PDF (723 kb)
ISBN: 1-4116-2383-5
Copyright Year: © 2005 by Samuel Blankson
Language: English
Publisher: Lulu.com

If you have ever wanted to know how to make money from real estate, but could never find one source that listed and explained all the different options available to you, then your search is over. This book covers over 20 different ways of investing in real estate. You will find the author's style easy to understand and very practical. The section on self-build is so in-depth, that after reading it you will actually know how to build a house, and the section on REITs, Indexes, and REIT Options will leave your mind boggling at the potential profits available to you. This book also covers the conversional and popular methods of real estate investing as well. Therefore, whether you want to learn to develop real estate projects, build your own home, or simply rent a room in your house, this book will help you maximise your success and avoid the pitfalls.

Making Money with Funds

Printed: 79 pages, 6.0 x 9.0 in., Perfect-bound
Download: PDF (8769 kb)
ISBN: 1-4116-2671-0
Copyright Year: © 2005 by Samuel Blankson
Language: English
Publisher: Lulu.com

Today the world fund market is a multi trillion-dollar industry. There are many types of funds and as many reasons for choosing them. In this book, you will learn how Funds work, and how you, can make money with them.

How to make a fortune on the Stock Markets

Printed: 190 pages, 8.5 x 11.0 in, Perfect-bound
Download: PDF (8769 kb)
ISBN: 1-4116-2379-7
Copyright Year: © 2005 by Samuel Blankson
Language: English
Publisher: Lulu.com

This book contains simple but effective techniques for achieving regular and consistent profits from stock trading. Unlike other books on the topic, it is not full of theory and projections, but practical advice learned the hard way, by trading personal hard-earned cash daily in the world's stock exchanges. Moreover, unlike other books on the subject, it is not about how to be a stock trader and trade other people's money, but on how to grow your own funds to a level where you will never have to work for anyone else again. This book contains real techniques used by the author to amass a fortune significant enough to have made him Financially Free. Now you too can use these simple but highly effective techniques to achieve the same results. Therefore, whether you are a professional trader or a total beginner, this book will show you how to achieve Financial Freedom through trading Stocks and Shares.

How to make a fortune with Options trading

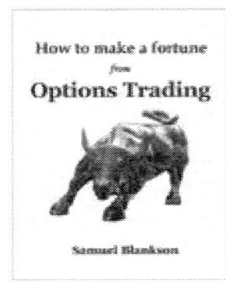

Printed: 59 pages, 8.5 x 11.0 in, Perfect-bound
Download: PDF (1808 kb)
ISBN: 1-4116-2378-9
Copyright Year: © 2005 by Samuel Blankson
Language: English
Publisher: Lulu.com

This is a practical book on winning in the Options trading market. Whether you are a sophisticated investor or a complete novice, this book is for you. The author takes complex ideas, and explains them in a way that is both practical and easily understood by anyone. Having used these techniques to achieve financial freedom, Mr Blankson now shares with you how he did it. There is no waffling here, just plain speaking and powerful techniques that anyone can apply.

Tax Avoidance A practical guide for UK residents

Printed: 104 pages, 6.0 x 9.0 in, Perfect-bound
Download: PDF (355 kb)
ISBN: 1-4116-2380-0
Copyright Year: © 2005 by Samuel Blankson
Language: English
Publisher: Lulu.com

UK residents pay some of the highest taxes in the world. Most of these taxes are hidden through VAT and service charges. This guide clearly explains what taxes you are paying, and which ones you can and should avoid paying through claiming your allowed deductions and allowances. Prudent tax efficient estate planning is explained in detail, and hundreds of tax saving ideas are shared within these pages. Whether you are a qualified accountant or a non-professional, you will find this little guide an invaluable source of tax saving ideas and strategies.

The Ultimate Guide to Offshore Tax Havens

Printed: 418 pages, 8.5 x 11.0 in, Perfect-bound
Download: PDF (12602 kb)
ISBN: 1-4116-2384-3
Copyright Year: © 2005 by Samuel Blankson
Language: English
Publisher: Lulu.com

This book is a detailed listing of all the known and not so commonly known Tax Havens, their benefits, and their suitability for relocation by the low tax seeker. If you are looking for ways to cut your taxes, there is no better way than to relocate to a low or no tax haven. The South East Asian Tsunamis and earthquakes have shown us that it is prudent to select the haven you will reside in carefully. Low taxes cannot be your only gauge for this task. This book will help you make that decision.

A must read for all who aspire to changing their lifestyles by relocating offshore. The havens are listed in geographical order, starting with the USA and ending with the South Pacific Islands.

Attitude

Printed: 418 pages, 6.0 x 9.0 in, Perfect-bound
Download: PDF (13700 kb)
ISBN: 1-4116-2382-7
Copyright Year: © 2005 by Samuel Blankson
Language: English
Publisher: Lulu.com

Attitude, so often misunderstood, yet so vital for success in every aspect of our lives. A positive attitude will guarantee happiness in your life, promotion and growth in your career or job, peace and joy in your family life, and in addition, a positive attitude has been scientifically proven to help extend your life expectancy. In this book, this essential success attribute is explained in detail. You will learn how to safeguard against positive attitude erosion, and learn how to build a positive mental attitude to help you achieve measurable success in every aspect of your life.

How to win at Greyhound betting

Printed: 68 pages, 8.5 x 11.0 in, Perfect-bound
Download: PDF (639 kb)
ISBN: 1-4116-2377-0
Copyright Year: © 2005 by Samuel Blankson
Language: English
Publisher: Lulu.com

Today, sports betting is a big industry for the bookmakers and organisers. Of all the people who benefit from sports racing, the "punters" (or in this case, you), are the last on the list of people who consistently gain. In fact, the greyhounds probably gain more from these races than most punters. Why is that? Well, there are many reasons, but most of them centre on these two things: lack of a proven system, and greed. This book closely examines these two points, and offers techniques and systems for achieving consistent wins in greyhound betting.

The Ultimate Greyhound Betting System

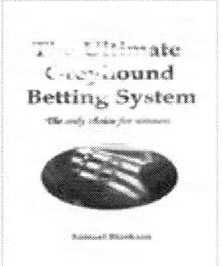

Download: MS Excel (233 kb)
Copyright Year: © 2005 by Samuel Blankson
Language: English
Publisher: Lulu.com

If you think there is no trustworthy betting system out there, then prepare to be proven wrong. This is the betting system described in the series *The Practical Guide to Total Financial Freedom,* and the book *How to win at Greyhound betting.* This semi-automatic system allows its user to achieve a minimum of 30% profits per week by following a proven statistical and rule based system betting on UK Greyhound races. The system only requires you to supply the race results and place the bets with your bookmaker. Armed with this incredible system, you will be able to beat the odds, and win one over the bookmakers.

How to Win at Online Roulette

Printed: 81 pages, 6.0 x 9.0 in, Perfect-bound
ISBN: 1-4116-2570-6
Copyright Year: © 2005 by Samuel Blankson
Language: English
Publisher: Lulu.com

This is a guide to consistently winning at online Roulette. It is a simple and to the point writing about an amazing system for gaining an advantage at online Casinos. This book will show you how to make £1000 per day or more from online Roulette.

Sixty Original Song Lyrics

Printed: 200 pages, 6.0 x 9.0 in, Perfect-bound
Download: PDF (1072 kb)
ISBN: 1-4116-2059-3
Copyright Year: © 2004 by Samuel Blankson
Language: English
Publisher: Lulu.com

This is a compilation of original song lyrics by Samuel Blankson. This book contains 60 of the songs he wrote in between 2000 – 2002. Having had some of these lyrics made into songs for an album (see *www.practicalbooks.org*), and several of them now on compilations, Samuel now shares these 60 song lyrics with you.

Images of Kilimanjaro

Printed: 26 pages, 11 x 8.5 in, Coil-bound
Start Date: January 1st, 2006
Duration: 12 months
Copyright Year: © 2004 by Samuel Blankson
Language: English
Publisher: Lulu.com

Kilimanjaro, the tallest freestanding mountain in the world, is captured here for you to feast your eyes on each month through 2006. Kilimanjaro is a source of life for Tanzania and Kenya locals, who live on its life giving rains and water. I had the honour of climbing this majestic mountain, and captured the essence of its allure and mystery through these pictures.

Images of Kilimanjaro

Printed: 53 pages, 8.5 x 11.0 in, Perfect-bound
Download: PDF (2573 kb)
ISBN: 1-4116-2016-X
Copyright Year: © 2004
Language: English
Publisher: Lulu.com

This is a book of pictures taken from Kilimanjaro. This is an accompanying book to the Calendar of the same name.

Uju

Download: MPG (6523 kb)
UPC: 4-3157-3526-2
Copyright Year: © 2004 by Samuel and Uju Blankson
Language: English
Publisher: Lulu.com

A six track EP with soulful R&B tracks with a pop flavour. This EP is bound to have you humming along addictively. For more info about the artist Uju, visit *www.uju-music.com* and look out for her forthcoming album.

The Bass by Samuel Blankson

Download: MPG (4811 kb)
Copyright Year: © 2004 by Samuel and Uju Blankson
Language: English
Publisher: Lulu.com

A sexy, R&B track with wicked beats and a deep baseline. With a melody and chorus that will stay with you for a long time, this addictive and catchy tune deserves your download (see *www.practicalbooks.org*).

Investing in En Primeur Wine

Printed: 88 pages, 6.0 x 9.0 in, Perfect-bound
Download: PDF (1,095 kb)
ISBN: 1-4116-2867-5
Copyright Year: © 2005
Language: English
Publisher: Lulu.com

Wine investing is not new, it has been going on for centuries. In more recent years (the last two centuries), government tax laws on alcoholic drinks have made buying wine a little more prohibitive to the investor who wants to keep them at home in his/her private cellar. Nevertheless, as usual, the market has found a way around this problem.

You can avoid taxes and V.A.T. (Value Added Tax) by buying fine wine on Bond (also called wine Futures or En Primeur). This book covers a simple and effective way in which anybody coming into the fine wine investing market place can safely securely and successfully select, and invest in En Primeur Wine.

Eight Steps to Success

Printed: 105 pages, 6.0 x 9.0 in, Perfect-bound
Download: PDF (1,095 kb)
ISBN: 1-4116-2738-5
Copyright Year: © 2005
Language: English
Publisher: Lulu.com

We would all like to live a successful life, a life where our relationships and finances are a source of happiness and joy. This life is attainable by following timeless success principles. These principles have been forgotten by our fast food, fast-paced, reality TV society.

This book defines, explains, and shows you how to apply these principles and skills in your life to attain happiness, contentment, peace, joy, and prosperity. The eight fundamental virtues and skills required to succeed long-term in any endeavour, are explained in detail and in a style that everyone can understand and immediately apply.

The Eight Steps to Success is an inspirational book that will help you understand, acquire, hone, and apply the principles of success.

Taking Action

Printed: 105 pages, 6.0 x 9.0 in, Perfect-bound
Download: PDF (1,095 kb)
ISBN: 1-4116-2735-0
Copyright Year: © 2005
Language: English
Publisher: Lulu.com

This is a book about taking action. For some, taking action means something you will do, might do, should do, have done, or never will do. This book will show you how to change your understanding of taking action to mean something you are doing NOW! When you change this focus in your life, you will release great powers. This book will show you how to tap into this phenomenal power and change your life.

About The Author

An entrepreneur at heart, Samuel Blankson blends art, creativity, passion, business acumen, and financial expertise with careful planning and execution in the achievement of measurable results. He is an avid reader, writer, researcher, and securities trader.

He is an advocate of self-empowerment and an individual's ability to control their destiny through the achievement of personal freedom from economic, financial, spiritual, social, mental, and interrelationship restrictions. Samuel is constantly working to push the boundaries of personal achievements to their limits, recognising that these limits are only self-imposed.

Samuel has authored over twenty books (*How to Destroy Your Debts*, *Living the Ultimate Truth*, *Developing Personal Integrity*, *The Practical Guide to Total Financial Freedom* volumes 1, 2, 3, 4 and 5, and *Attitude* are some of these works). He has written over 100 songs, sixty of which are featured in *Sixty Original Song Lyrics*. He writes poetry, creates artwork, and works daily to express his creativity in many ways.

Having successfully run several businesses, Samuel diversified into securities trading over a decade ago, with great success. After learning from the masters of the time, Samuel progressed to develop his own methods and systems for successful trading. Today, he trades many financial instruments and has developed ways of successfully generating profits from his many investments.

A firm believer in knowledge sharing, Samuel travels the globe, teaching and sharing his personal knowledge with groups of friends, associates, and anyone who seeks to improve their life. This is the spirit of Samuel Blankson, a God centred philanthropist, overcomer, and high achiever.

Printed in Great Britain
by Amazon

82355447R00077